YOU CAN BE A
magician

harold
philmore
wells

Member of
SOUTHEASTERN MAGICIANS ASSOCIATION

MOODY PRESS
CHICAGO

© 1976 by
THE MOODY BIBLE INSTITUTE
OF CHICAGO

Library of Congress Cataloging in Publication Data

Wells, Harold Philmore.
  You can be a magician!

  1. Christian education—Audio-visual aids.
2. Preaching. I. Title.
BV4227.W44   207   75-35535
ISBN 0-8024-9823-X

Printed in the United States of America

CONTENTS

PART III—PAPER-TEARING

PART IV—USEFUL PROPS

In loving memory of my father,
SAMUEL G. WELLS,
who, through his quiet example,
taught me much about Christ
and His love

And that from a child thou hast
known the Holy Scriptures, which
are able to M ake thee wise
unto s A lvation
throu G h faith
wh I ch
is in C hrist Jesus.
2 Timothy 3:15

INTRODUCTION

Magic appeals to children and adults alike because it is mystifying. It arouses our curiosity. Thus, in the hand of the religious worker, magic becomes a very important tool in conveying the great spiritual truths of God's eternal Word.

One of the problems with the use of any new or different method of teaching is that many people are afraid to launch out and give it an honest try. Perhaps the main reason for this is that people often feel that they are not talented enough to learn and utilize something so strangely new and seemingly complicated. Or they may lack the self-confidence and courage necessary to just step out and experiment with new media of teaching.

Therefore, let me set you at ease before we go any further by stating that I am convinced that anyone who really loves teaching the Word of God and the individuals with whom they work, *can* skillfully and competently learn to use magic as an effective tool in presenting spiritual truths. I receive letters regularly from ministers, Sunday school teachers, missionaries, and religious workers around the world, who, because of their earnest desire to find a more effective method of teaching and by simply following the instructions, have found magic to be one of the most effective and fascinating methods of teaching they have ever used. You too will find, once you have witnessed the results of such presentations, that the effort and time spent in preparing yourself to use magic to illustrate biblical truths was well worth it.

7

You see, sermons in magic are tremendously effective because a child, or adult for that matter, rarely forgets what he sees, especially when the element of mystery is present. The familiar saying, "In one ear and out the other," is often true. However, have you ever heard anyone make the statement, "In one eye and out the other"? No, for it is a proven fact that the mind retains that which it sees long after the spoken word alone is forgotten. Thus magic becomes a valuable visual hook upon which the child can mentally hang the essential spiritual truths which have been taught. Through sermons in magic, the message presented enters both the eye and the ear, making it a tremendously effective teaching tool.

Visual aids as a medium of teaching is by no means new. God Himself was the first to use this wonderful and effective method of teaching. You will recall how, after the Flood, God set a rainbow in the sky as a visual confirmation of His covenant with mankind (Gen 9). Another visual sermon was the memorial built by the people of Israel after they had crossed the Jordan River. A man from each tribe took a stone out of the river and placed it where they lodged. Then Joshua said to them, "This may be a sign among you, that when your children ask their fathers in time to come, saying, What mean ye by these stones? Then ye shall answer them" (Jos 4:6-7).

As you study the Old Testament prophets, you will find that often God directed them to perform symbolic acts that were nothing more than effective perceptual sermons to present to God's people His divine message. Through this skillful technique, the people of Israel more easily understood and remembered the spiritual truths God wished to convey to them through His prophets.

As one examines the gospels, he cannot help but be impressed by the way Jesus Christ used this graphic style of teaching in order to convey His message to the multitudes. In fact, the Church today still uses two of His visual sermons: baptism and the Lord's Supper. So one can readily see that the Old and New

Testaments are filled with visual sermons or object lessons as a dexterous manner of presenting the message of God to mankind.

Visual sermons can help you to make the teaching-learning process more accurate, interesting, and permanent. This is especially true with relation to object lessons with magic.

However, let me stress as forcefully as I can, for any sermon in magic to be truly effective, one must keep in mind an important and essential truth, namely, the magical effect must *never* become an end in itself, but *must* at all times be only a means to an end. The *only* purpose for the magic effect is to create interest and to illustrate visually the spiritual truth you are seeking to impart to your audience. Always keep foremost in your mind that the magic you perform is merely a window to allow the light of God's truth to enter the mind of your congregation. You will never go astray in your use of magic in sermon illustration if you remember that it is only the medium through which you convey a message to your viewers. *Never* lose sight of the fact that it is the message that must at all times be uppermost in your presentation of sermons in magic. You will have been a miserable failure if all your congregation can remember after you have finished your sermon in magic is the effect you performed. However, you will have been successful if the effect is remembered as a mental hook upon which your audience has hung the spiritual truth.

A word of caution: *Don't* fall into the old trap of thinking that visual aids are a means of helping the teacher get by with little or no preparation. To be skillful in the use of visual aids, but more especially in magic, a tremendous amount of preparation is necessary. The performance of magic is not easy. Each effect must be mastered if it is to be done effectively and convincingly. This will take a lot of time and patience. THERE IS NO SHORT-CUT TO SUCCESS IN THIS FIELD!

Much thought and preparation must go into not only the presentation of the magical effect but also the sermon content itself. Unless you have thoroughly prepared your talk, with the magical effect merely as illustrative impact, you have wasted your time and that of your audience. Also, it is not to be used for entertainment but to facilitate conveying spiritual truths. You are not in front of your congregation in order to show off your wonderful talent to mystify and entertain. You are before them, as a servant of God, to present an important message from the eternal Word of God.

SUGGESTIONS FOR IDEAS THAT MAY BE USED AS SERMONS IN MAGIC

In the pages that follow, you will find a number of tested suggestions that you may find helpful in creating sermons in magic. You may not wish to use the message exactly as suggested; but, through studying the effect, you may be stimulated with ideas of how you may more effectively use the effect to prepare a message of your own. To get across the message you wish to present, you must adapt each effect to your own personality. The main purpose of this book is to open up for you new avenues of creative thinking in the field of magic to illustrate biblical truths.

There is no doubt in my mind that if you will use this wonderful method of visual education, you will find that your effectiveness in presenting the Word of God to children will be greatly enhanced. The time and energy you spend in developing your technique in presenting sermons in magic will be personally rewarding and will greatly increase your ability to touch the lives of countless people with the wonderful message of salvation through faith in Jesus Christ our risen Lord.

These suggestions for sermons in magic are shared with you in the hope that your effectiveness in the presentation of the glorious truths of Christ will be tremendously enhanced. Read through them carefully; think creatively, and rich blessings and rewards await you through the use of this medium.

PART I

PREPARATION

1

GUIDELINES FOR THE USE OF MAGIC IN SERMONS

FROM MY OWN EXPERIENCE in the presentation of sermons in magic, I would like to share with you some essential and basic guidelines that will help you as you launch out into this area of visual education. Each of these suggestions is important to the effective presentation of magic in illustrating spiritual truth; so please study them carefully. If you will follow these simple guidelines, you will find this method of teaching both personally rewarding and an effective tool in teaching the Word of God.

1. Never attempt even the most simple effect until you have spent sufficient time practicing it and feel really comfortable in your ability to perform it effectively.
2. Remember, you are presenting a spiritual message. Thus, spend time in meditation and prayer before each performance. You will need the leadership of the Holy Spirit if the truths of God's Word are to penetrate the hearts of your listeners. Ask Him to work through you in using the magical effect simply as a hook upon which your congregation will be able to mentally hang the spiritual truth of your message.
3. Make sure that each piece of equipment used is in its proper place and is in good working condition and appearance. *Never* take it for granted that a piece of equipment

is all set and ready to go. Check and double check before each performance in order to eliminate possible embarrassment and distraction.

4. Rehearse your message! Not only to be sure of its content but to know where in the message the magic will be most effective. Rehearse before a mirror so that you can see the effect from the audience's point of view. Rehearsing in this manner will also reveal to you any clumsy moves you might still be making. If you have small children at home, practice your message and effect before them. They will enjoy it, and you will also be able to see if you have perfected the magical effect. You might also ask for feedback from them as to what was the central thought in your message. This will give you a good idea as to whether your message is simple enough to be easily understood.

5. When presenting sermons in magic, *do not talk down* to your audience. Beware of using a soft, pious sounding, or fairy-tale type voice.

6. *Never* give the impression that you think you are superior to your audience or that you possess some special talent or supernatural power. Keep uppermost in your mind that you are not there for the purpose of astounding them with your magical prowess. Your main purpose in being there is to teach them an important truth from God's eternal Word. Be sure that you are always on guard against a "look-what-I-can-do" facial or bodily expression or attitude.

7. Remember, you are not putting on an entertainment program per se. Your primary reason for being before the audience is to present God's Word. You are His representative, His messenger. Therefore, at all times, you should maintain an atmosphere of dignity and reverence. If you don't, you will encourage the children present to get out of hand, and the overall effectiveness of your message and presentation will be lost.

8. Avoid audience participation, because it most likely will result in some children screaming for your attention and others running and fighting to get to the platform to assist you with some effect. If the magic effect being used requires assistance, choose those you wish to assist you well in advance of the start of the service.

9. Avoid embarrassing your audience, or you will destroy the ultimate purpose of the magic. Some magicians might disagree with me on this point, but from personal experience, I am convinced that any magical effect with a "sucker" ending should *never* be used in the presentation of sermons. For entertainment purposes these types of effects are great, but are out of place in the pulpit or religious education classroom.

10. Never rush through an effect. On the other hand, do not purposely draw it out too long. Make sure that just enough time is spent in order to show the effect clearly and to explain each step as you go along so that everyone understands exactly what is taking place. Unless they are fully aware of what is taking place, the effectiveness of your message will be lost.

11. If you *must* use theological terms in your message, be sure to take the time necessary to fully explain in simple, everyday language what they mean. *Don't* ever take it for granted that your audience knows the meaning of such terms as *redemption, atonement, incarnation, born again.* Avoid, if at all possible, the use of large, technical, and theological words. This is especially true when your audience is mainly children. In fact, this is a good idea even when talking to the average adult audience.

12. Never let your equipment lie around so that it can be handled and examined by the audience. When you have finished with an effect, put it away. Have a standing rule that *no one* is to come up on the platform following the service.

13. Be sure that the props being used are large enough to be seen from all parts of the room or auditorium. If at all possible, use a platform with a backdrop of some sort. Also be sure that the area is well lighted, with the lights above you and in front of you. Do *not* have lights behind you.

14. *Never* reveal the secret of a magic effect to anyone. Christian workers certainly ought to be ethical in this particular respect. There are many individuals who make their livelihood by the art of illusion. Therefore, have enough respect for them and their craft not to destroy its effectiveness by revealing its secrets. Children as well as the adults will try to get you to explain to them how a certain effect was done, but *don't* give in; stand your ground. Believe me, they'll respect you for it. While we're on this subject, let me urge you not to lay this book around for others to pick up and glance through merely to satisfy their curiosity.

15. Always radiate an atmosphere of enjoyment while giving a sermon in magic. In working with children especially, your personality will speak more loudly than your voice. Let them know through your facial expressions and the tone of your voice that what you are about to say and do is tremendously important. Let them sense, by your actions and expression, that you are really happy to be with them. Radiate enthusiasm! Never give the impression through non-verbal communication that you are bored.

16. Last, but by no means least, if you don't have a real love for magic and children, *don't* use this medium as a means of visual education. You will quickly find that if children think they know how a particular magic effect is done, they have a natural tendency to blurt out, "Oh, I know how that's done!" When such a moment occurs, always remember that most children are not mean and do not purposely wish to embarrass you. Don't let them unnerve you. Don't

show any signs of disgust, anger, or displeasure. Exhibit to your audience at all times a truly Christian spirit. Anticipate such interruptions, and then you will not be disturbed by them. When they arise—and they will—just calmly go on with your sermon and magic effect.

2

ARRANGING A ROOM OR AUDITORIUM

CERTAIN MAGIC EFFECTS require certain precautions with reference to where you will stand to perform, the position of the audience, lights, windows, and so on.

A short distance should be kept between you and the audience. This will prevent them from seeing around the sides of you. If at all possible, you should be on a platform so that you are high enough above the audience to be seen by all present. It is important that the audience be able to see every move that you make, that they understand at all times what is taking place. Height of the platform and angles of performer to audience are tremendously important. Your hand or a piece of equipment held at the wrong angle can easily give the secret of the effect away, thus destroying its usefulness.

In addition, if you have a small shelf behind your table for the purpose of disposing of articles or for loading an apparatus, it is very important that you are not too near your audience. Study figure 1 to see what I mean about distance and angles.

Most individuals are sensible enough to understand and appreciate that anyone performing magic effects needs to be a short distance from them and that the audience must always be in front of the performer and not on the sides.

If you are doing more than one magic effect, be sure not to litter your table with too much equipment. Keep the table neat and orderly. Keep additional pieces of equipment and odds and ends on a separate table and bring them over as you require them. If you have any special items, conceal them beneath a colored silk or behind a card screen, so that their effect will not be lost when the audience sees them for the first time. In all magic effects, the rule of thumb is always use the element of surprise.

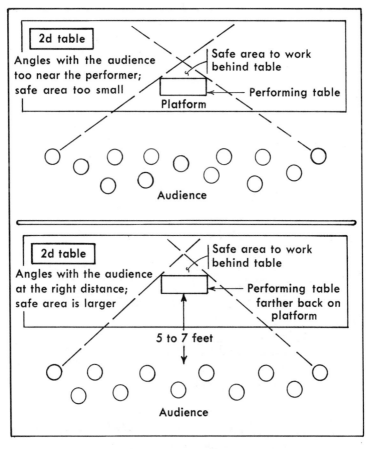

Fig. 1. Position of magician and audience

PART II

VISUAL SERMONS

3

DIRECTED BY GOD

Text: Numbers 9:15-23

MATERIALS

A round or square piece of wood with a hole bored through it (see fig. 2)

A piece of rope large enough in diameter to move smoothly through the hole. It should be approximately 3 feet in length.

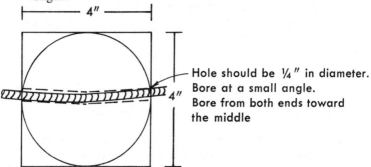

Hole should be ¼" in diameter.
Bore at a small angle.
Bore from both ends toward the middle

Fig. 2. Preparing the block of wood

EFFECT

The square or round piece of wood is shown threaded on the rope which runs freely through it. At your command the piece of wood can be stopped or started moving down the rope.

By relieving the tension on the rope, the piece of wood will move slowly down the rope. When you wish to stop it, merely pull tightly on the ends of the rope, putting tension on it. This will cause it to stop, because the rope will bind at the point where the two bored holes meet at the center of the block of wood. When the block has moved all the way to the bottom of the rope, turn the rope over placing the block at the top of the rope (see fig. 3). This may be done as many times as necessary in order to illustrate your message.

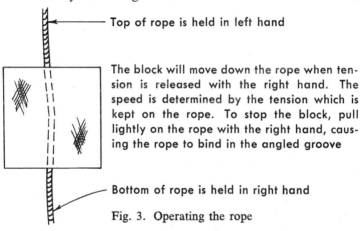

Top of rope is held in left hand

The block will move down the rope when tension is released with the right hand. The speed is determined by the tension which is kept on the rope. To stop the block, pull lightly on the rope with the right hand, causing the rope to bind in the angled groove

Bottom of rope is held in right hand

Fig. 3. Operating the rope

MESSAGE

Tell the story of the children of Israel wandering in the wilderness and how God guided them to the promised land by the pillar of cloud by day and the pillar of fire by night. When the pillar of cloud or fire stopped, then the children of Israel were to do the same. When it moved, they followed it. Thus they were safely guided by the leadership of Almighty God.

As Christians we too should be submissive to the guidance of the Lord in our lives. We should daily seek His leadership. There will be times when we need to stop and spiritually renew

19

ourselves for the task ahead. But we must also be attuned to Him; so that we know when it is time to move out again to do His will. The committed Christian is daily directed by God. He is never in a hurry to move out ahead of God's leadership or slow to respond to His guidance. He is eager to know God's will for his life and quick to respond accordingly.

During the message, emphasize your point of responding to the will of God, demonstrating it by the response of the wood block to your command to stop or go.

4

GOD'S SAVING MIRACLE

Text: Romans 6:23

MATERIALS

A table covered with a felt pad or equivalent
Base with dowel
Four cubes
One tube (see fig. 4)
A soft felt hat large enough to cover one of the cubes

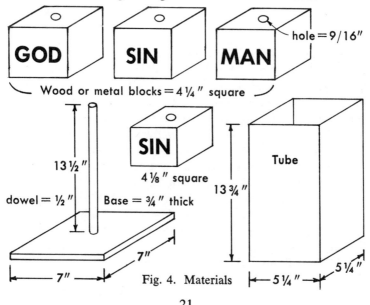

Fig. 4. Materials

Tube and base of stand are made of plywood. The tube of ¼ or ½ inch; the base of ¾ inch. The cubes can be made of any material, but thin laminated wood or tin is best. The tops and insides of all four cubes should be painted flat black so that, if you happen to tilt one of the cubes too much, the audience will not notice that the cubes are hollow. They should appear as solid wooden blocks. The cube representing God should be painted white to represent the purity and holiness of God. The letters should be approximately 2 inches high and painted black for good visibility. The cubes representing sin should be painted dark blue or black to represent the awfulness of sin in the sight of God. Paint the letters S-I-N white, approximately 2 inches high. The cube representing man should be painted gray, as man was created in the image of God but lacked the full purity and holiness of God. Paint the letters M-A-N white, two inches high. The tube is painted red to represent the blood of Christ. The base should be painted any bright color such as blue or yellow.

Effect

The cubes marked SIN are on the table with the 4⅛ inch cube inside the 4¼ inch cube. A felt hat is placed over them for a moment while the cube marked GOD is placed on the base, and the cube marked MAN is placed on top of it. Be sure that the cubes are stacked at angles to each other (see fig. 5). The cube marked MAN is removed from the base at the same time that the felt hat is lifted from the cubes marked SIN. (As this is being done with the right hand, be sure to press tightly through the felt hat and grip the 4¼ inch cube and lift it off the 4⅛ inch cube.) The 4⅛ inch cube, SIN, is then placed on the cube, GOD, then the cube, MAN, is placed on top of it. The red tube is placed over the three cubes. When the tube is removed, only two cubes, GOD and MAN, are on the base. The cube, SIN, has mysteriously disappeared. The felt hat is then lifted to reveal the cube marked SIN.

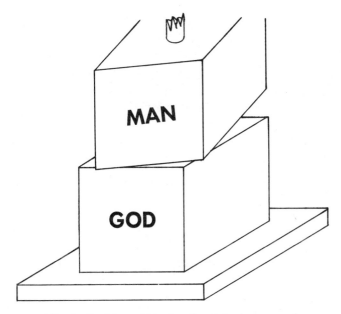

Fig. 5. Position of blocks after tube is removed

How to Perform the Effect

Set up the equipment on the table to be used with the tube and base stand and blocks on one side, the felt hat on the other. It is advisable to have a pad or cloth over the top of the table so that the sounds of moving the blocks will be muffled. Then follow the directions in the paragraphs above.

Message

The message is the Gospel, based on Romans 6:23. This effect is a marvelous visual aid for the presentation of the plan of salvation. Starting with the story of the Fall of man in Genesis, proceed to elaborate on sin and its consequences. The heart of the message is that sin separates man from God, but because of God's great love (Jn 3:16), He has provided a way whereby we can be reconciled to Him. The plan of God involved the gift

23

of His Son, Jesus Christ. He came and died on Calvary in our behalf, and through our faith in Him, our sin is removed. At the conclusion of the effect, as you pick up the felt hat to show the block marked SIN, quote Psalm 103:11-12.

How much detail you give depends on the amount of time you have for the sermon. Don't rush it! Tell enough of the story of man's Fall and God's plan to redeem man that your audience fully understands the plan of salvation. Keep it simple, and let the effect assist you in telling this important truth.

5

THE STRANGE APPEARANCE
OF CHRIST

Text: John 20:26

MATERIALS

A large bottle with a neck large enough to hold a cork approximately 1½ inches in diameter

A large cork that will fit tightly into the neck of the bottle

A small, silk handkerchief (12 inches square)

A small piece of natural colored thread

A small button

A silk handkerchief large enough to completely cover the bottle

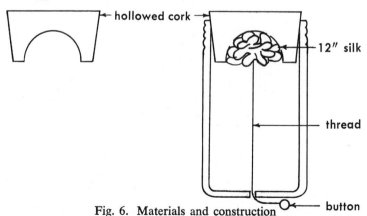

Fig. 6. Materials and construction

Hollow out the cork with a sharp knife from the bottom side (see fig. 6). Make sure the hole is large enough to completely conceal the 12-inch handkerchief. If you do not have a high speed drill, take the bottle to a jeweler and have him drill a hole $\frac{1}{16}$ inch in diameter in the center of the bottom of the bottle. Tie a piece of thin, natural colored thread to one end of the silk handkerchief. Run the thread through the hole in the bottom of the jar and tie a small button to the end of the thread (see fig. 6).

EFFECT

A tightly corked bottle is shown empty to the audience. A large handkerchief is thrown over the bottle completely covering it. When the handkerchief is removed, a silk has mysteriously appeared inside the still tightly corked bottle.

HOW TO PERFORM THE EFFECT

Place the bottle on the table with the thread and button toward the back of the bottle and away from the audience. (The silk is already concealed in the cork in the bottle.) Point to the jar and explain that it is empty and tightly corked. Place the large silk handkerchief over the bottle completely covering it. After you have draped the silk over the bottle, pick it up with the left hand at the top. Then, with the right hand, reach under the silk as if to adjust the bottle so that it is completely covered by the silk. At this moment, pull slightly on the button attached to the thread, pulling the silk out of the cork into the bottom of the bottle. Place the bottle back on the table. The bottle is now prepared for the conclusion of the effect.

MESSAGE

Tell the story recorded in John 20. Use your imagination to describe the disciples sitting in the upper room, talking about the strange events which had taken place during the past week. Emphasize that all the doors and windows were locked tight.

However, in spite of the locked doors and windows, Christ appeared in their midst. Thomas, one of the twelve, was absent, and when the others told him of the appearance of Christ in the upper room, he just couldn't believe that Christ had risen. It was just impossible. Unless he could see Him and touch Him, he would not believe. Some eight days later, Thomas was with the other disciples when Christ again appeared. This time, Thomas drops to his knees and cries out, "My Lord and my God." At this point, read John 20:26. As you read this passage, lift the handkerchief that is covering the bottle.

From this point on, you can develop the sermon in many directions. You can speak on the importance of faith in one's life, or how doubt can rob one of so many wonderful blessings and joys in his life, or on the theme of how through Christ the impossible always becomes possible. During the Easter season you could develop the idea of the power of the resurrected Christ in the lives of people today.

6

HE IS ABLE TO KEEP YOU FROM FALLING

Text: 2 Peter 3:17-18; 1 Corinthians 15:58; Jude 21, 24

MATERIALS

A steel ball bearing about 1 inch in diameter

A magician's wand, made from a piece of ¾-inch or 1-inch doweling, with two metal or plastic tips 1 inch long on each end. Wand must be grooved as shown in figure 7.

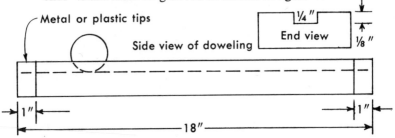

Fig. 7. Construction of the wand

CONSTRUCTION DATA

Take a piece of doweling approximately 18 inches long and cut a ¼-inch by ⅛-inch deep groove the full length of the dowel (see side view in fig. 7). Then place on both ends either metal or plastic tips. Paint the dowel black, and the tips should be white.

EFFECT

The wand is shown to the audience, the steel ball is placed on the wand, and an attempt is made to balance it on the wand, but it rolls off. However, with persistent effort, it finally mysteriously balances, and you are even able to let it roll back and forth across the top of the wand without its falling off.

How to Perform the Effect

Hold the wand in your left hand by the tip. Be *sure* the grooved edge of the wand is away from the audience and facing you so that the groove cannot be seen by the audience. Place the steel ball on the wand with the right hand and attempt to balance it on the wand. Remove your hand from the ball and catch it as it rolls off the wand. Do this a number of times as you are talking about the importance of stability in one's Christian life.

As you quote Jude 24, make a quarter of a turn of the wand so that the groove is now at the top. This should be done in such a manner as not to draw attention of the audience to the fact that the wand has been turned at all.

Now again make an attempt to balance the ball on the wand. Once it is balanced in the groove, slowly tip the wand so that the ball will roll down the wand. Do not let it roll all the way to the tip. After it has rolled a few inches, tip the wand in the opposite direction. After you have done this a few times, slowly tip the wand toward you, allowing the ball to fall off into your hand. *Be sure to keep the grooved edge of the wand away from the audience at all time.*

MESSAGE

Start by reading 2 Peter 3:17 aloud. Talk about how easy it is to lose one's stability in the Christian faith. Then go on to read 2 Peter 3:18, emphasizing how important it is to grow daily in the grace and knowledge of Christ. Point out that as we grow in spiritual maturity, we develop an inner power and stability necessary to cope with the temptations and crises life throws at us.

At this point, you might want to quote 1 Corinthians 15:58, placing emphasis on the need to learn to be steadfast, immovable in our Christian convictions. You could elaborate here on the importance of Bible study, prayer, church attendance, and Christian service in one's life, if he is to mature spiritually.

Then proceed to quote Jude 21, emphasizing the importance of keeping ourselves bathed in the love of God through Christ. (During this part of the sermon, you have been trying unsuccessfully to balance the steel ball on the wand. Through this effect, you are demonstrating to your audience how seemingly impossible a task it is.) State how difficult it is to live daily a victorious life but that it is possible through persistence and faith in Jesus Christ. Now place the ball on the wand. (This time you have turned the wand a quarter of a turn to place the grooved edge at the top.) With the ball in the groove, you are now able to balance it on the wand. Quote Jude 24 and proceed to tell the audience how through faith in Jesus Christ, all things are possible. The Christian life can be lived victoriously through the inner strength available to us through *faith*.

7

FAITH CAN REMOVE MOUNTAINS

Text: Matthew 17:20

MATERIALS

A piece of soft rope, approximately 36 inches long
A piece of solder, approximately 18 inches long

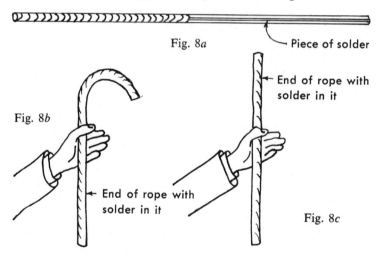

Fig. 8*a*

Piece of solder

End of rope with solder in it

Fig. 8*b*

End of rope with solder in it

Fig. 8*c*

Fig. 8. Position of the rope and solder

CONSTRUCTION DATA

Simply remove a few strands of the core of the soft rope, and, in its place, insert the piece of solder. Put a small amount of rubber cement or glue on the end of the solder to hold it in place.

A piece of rope is shown rolled up into a small coil. Slowly it is unrolled. Holding the rope in the middle, an attempt is made to make the rope rigid so that it will stand erect. After a few unsuccessful attempts, the seemingly impossible happens: the rope mysteriously stands erect.

How to Perform the Effect

The secret is to first let the half of the rope that has the solder in it dangle toward the floor (see fig. 8b). Hold the rope with the left hand at least an inch above the piece of solder, to give the effect that the entire bottom of the rope is limp like the top half. With the right hand, attempt to stretch the top half of the rope to make it stand erect. However, when it is turned loose, it will go limp.

When the moment arrives to illustrate your point, take the end of the rope that has the solder in it. Simply move the left hand down slightly and grip the end of the solder. Reach with the right hand and take hold of the end of the rope and stretch it taut. Quickly turn the ends of the rope so that the end with solder inserted in it is now at the top of the hand (see fig. 8c). Stretch it tight, and the rope will become rigid and stand erect without the aid of the right hand. (Take your time in stretching the rope so that you do not give the impression that it can be done so easily.) When you have completed the effect, roll the rope back into a small coil again and lay it on the table. The coil is used both before and after the effect to impress your audience with the fact that the rope is completely limp.

Message

Read Matthew 17:20 and then begin to talk about the tremendous power faith plays in our lives. Elaborate on the many mountains that we are called upon to face in our lives, such as temptations, sickness, hurts of all types and sizes, loneliness, and so on. Then proceed to explain how, through the inner strength available to us through faith in Jesus Christ, there is no mountain too large that it cannot be removed. At this point you may wish to illustrate from your own life or the lives of other people how, through faith, what seemed to be mountains have been removed. Faith always puts an *"I can"* into our lives. (At this point, ask the audience if they believe that it's possible to take a limp piece of soft rope and, by merely stroking it, cause it to stand erect and rigid, that is, without the aid of wires or string. Proceed to demonstrate how impossible it appears. Yet, it can be done. Demonstrate by actually making the rope become rigid and stand erect (without any assistance from you).

Emphasize that there is nothing impossible in the life of a person whose faith is firm in Jesus Christ and who has committed himself wholeheartedly to Him. In closing, you may want to make reference to Philippians 4:13 and 19, concluding with, "You and Christ make an undefeatable team."

8

BE TRUTHFUL IN ALL THINGS

Text: Ephesians 4:25

MATERIALS

Two pieces of cardboard, one black and one white, shaped like those in figure 9. Size can vary and should be determined by the size of your audience. *Be sure* that they are large enough to be seen by the entire congregation.

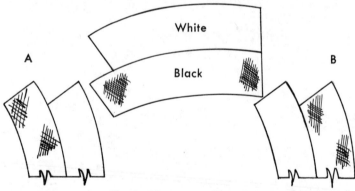

Fig. 9. The two cardboards

EFFECT

When the two pieces of cardboard are placed side by side, as in figure 9a, the black card appears to be larger than the white. If switched, as in figure 9b, the opposite appears to be true. However, if they are measured by placing them one on top of the other, it can be shown that they are exactly the same size.

MESSAGE

Begin your sermon by making reference to the common expression so often used about white lies. Many people think that it's all right to tell a white lie, because it never really hurts anyone. Therefore, it has become perfectly acceptable in most circles to tell a lie, provided it's a white one.

Continue by pointing out that, according to God's Word, there is no difference in the type of lies we tell. There is no such thing as a white or black lie in God's sight. His standard for us is that we be truthful in all things. Here you may wish to quote Ephesians 4:25.

Illustrate what you mean by showing the cards in figure 9a. Ask which appears to be the largest. Then after elaborating on the idea that many people have, that a white lie is always smaller than a black lie, switch the cards as in figure 9b. Now ask which appears to be the largest.

Continue by proving that although they appear larger, depending on which card is in front of the other, they are actually the same exact size. Prove this to the audience by placing the two cards on top of each other, showing that they are exactly the same in size.

Conclude by pointing out that this is true in everyday life. We must be truthful in all our dealings and relationships. We must not allow ourselves to be fooled into thinking that a so-called white lie or small falsehood is OK. Drive home the point that in all dealings, with others and ourselves, there must at all times be outright truthfulness and honesty.

You may want to make a large number of miniature cards to pass out to your audience after the service. They will act as a reminder and an incentive for them to become walking witnesses for Christ in their daily relationships with others.

9

CHAMELEON CHRISTIANS

Text: James 1:8

MATERIALS

A magical effect sold by all magic dealers under the name of the Color Changing Hank; it is very reasonable in price and gives a beautiful, colorful effect.

EFFECT

Performer exhibits a beautiful red silk. His hands are shown to be empty. The silk is held in the left hand, and when the right hand strokes the silk, it is seen to change to an entirely different color (see fig. 10). Immediately it can be changed back to its original color. This is a self-contained trick and does not require sleight of hand.

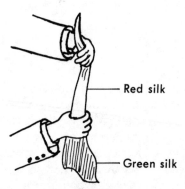

Fig. 10. Color Changing Hank

Your message should be centered around the importance of being a stable, single-minded Christian. Point out how easy it is to be a "chameleon" Christian. Explain at this point what chameleons are, how they have the unusual ability to change the color of their skin to match that of their environment. Continue by stating that there are many Christians who appear to have this same ability but do not possess the deep spiritual strength necessary to stand for what they believe no matter who they are with. When they are around Christians, they look, act, and talk as a Christian should, but when they are around others who do not profess faith in Jesus Christ, they soon begin to look, act, and talk as they do. Refer to James 1:8, where it says, a "double-minded man is unstable in all his ways."

Illustrate your message at this point by changing the colors of the Color-Changing Hank a number of times. Admonish your audience not to be fickle but firm in their convictions, to develop, through the strength and grace of God, a strong, stable Christian character. Encourage them to endeavor to be truly Christian wherever and with whomever they may be. To be the Christian Christ would have them to be, they must be consistent in their Christian walk at their work, school, and play, as well as church.

This same effect could be used to deliver a sermon in magic on being unstable and double-minded in one's doctrines. Such texts as Ephesians 4:14, Hebrews 13:9, James 1:6 might be used as springboards.

10

THE REDEMPTIVE POWER OF GOD

Text: Isaiah 1:18

MATERIALS

A change bag, as shown in figure 11
2 silks, a red one and a white one; they can either be 6 or 12 inches square.

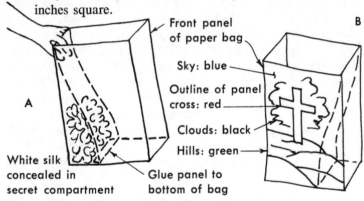

A — Front panel of paper bag

White silk concealed in secret compartment

Glue panel to bottom of bag

B — Sky: blue

Outline of panel cross: red

Clouds: black

Hills: green

Fig. 11. The change bag

CONSTRUCTION DATA

Take two 5-pound grocery bags, carefully cut the front and back panels from one of the bags. Discard the bottom and small folded sides. Take one of the panels, fold the bottom edge back about ½ inch. Insert this panel into the other bag and glue it securely in the middle of the bottom of the bag (see fig. 11a).

If you happen to be artistic, you might wish to make the change bag more attractive by painting the front panel of the bag as shown in figure 11*b* or to your own liking.

EFFECT

A common grocery bag is shown to be empty by your turning it upside down. A red silk is placed in the bag and immediately a white silk is taken out and the bag is again shown to be empty. The silk has mysteriously changed colors.

HOW TO PERFORM THE EFFECT

The bag is held with the fingertips of the left hand slightly inside the mouth of the bag, holding the secret panel closed tight against the side of the bag, thereby perfectly concealing the white silk that is hidden behind the panel (see fig. 11*a*). After the red silk has been placed inside the bag with the right hand, release the panel flap and switch the bag from the left to the right hand. Immediately secure the bag with the fingertips of the right hand, making sure that the index finger grips the secret panel pulling it tightly to the edge of the bag. In so doing the white silk is revealed and the red silk is now concealed behind the panel flap. After producing the white silk, you can now again show that the bag is empty.

MESSAGE

Explain that the bag (*do not* refer to it as a "change bag" but as a common paper sack or bag) represents the atoning work of Christ on Calvary for the salvation of mankind. The two silks, red and white, will be used to illustrate the wonderful message found in Isaiah 1:18. As you show the audience the bag, tell them the story of how God created man in His own image. However, man deliberately disobeyed God, and, as a result sin came into the world.

Continue by telling of God's love and concern for fallen man and how, immediately after man rebelled, God began to provide a redemptive plan whereby mankind could once again be reconciled unto Him. You might refer here to such Scriptures as John 3:16 and John 5:24. Then, as you talk of sinful man and his need to be redeemed, place the red silk in the bag. Refer here to your text, "red, as crimson."

Continue with the story of redemption. Conclude by quoting the last part of Isaiah 1:18, "They shall be as white as snow." At this point, pull the white silk out of the bag, showing that the red silk has been transformed into the white one, thus illustrating the wonderful and glorious truth that, through faith in Jesus Christ our Lord, our sins are washed away and we are redeemed and reconciled into full fellowship with God.

This change bag can be used for many sermons in magic. Do some creative thinking and you'll come up with some wonderful uses for it.

11

A SIN UNTO DEATH

Text: Joshua 7

MATERIALS

A change bag (the same type as illustrated in chapter 10, or a
professional one)

Three small silks, one yellow or gold, one silver or gray, and
one red; the red silk should be cut and hemmed in the shape
of a garment (see fig. 12a)

One large, black silk with the words, *Sin will find you out,*
printed on it (see fig. 12b)

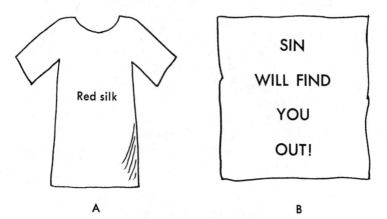

Fig. 12. The red and the black silks

The three silks are placed in the change bag after it has been shown to be empty. A large black silk with the words, *Sin will find you out,* printed on it is then removed from the bag. The three silks have mysteriously disappeared, and in their place the large silk appears.

How to Perform the Effect

Have the large black silk already concealed behind the panel in the change bag. As you tell the story drop each of the silks, representing what you are talking about in your sermon, into the bag. At the right moment, switch the bag from the left hand to the right hand, so as to switch the panel unnoticed, thus revealing the black silk. If you plan to use the type of change bag illustrated in chapter 10, be sure to reread the instructions in that sermon before doing this effect.

Message

Start by drawing the audience's attention to the change bag. It is to be used to represent Achan's tent. The silks (show them) are to be used to represent the various items which were to be consecrated unto the Lord and placed in the treasury.

Proceed to tell the story as recorded in Joshua 6 and 7. A good starting point is Joshua 6:18-19. God had made a covenant with His people Israel. He would be with them and they would be victorious, provided they followed His directions. However, if they disobeyed, then a curse would fall upon them and all the people would suffer. Under no circumstances were they to take for their personal use any of the spoils of battle. All of the spoils of battle were to be consecrated to God.

Continue by stating how Achan saw some things which he coveted. Thinking he could get away with secretly stealing just a few items, he stole them and hid them in the earth in the middle of his tent. The items he stole were a Babylonian garment (place the red silk cut in the shape of a garment into the bag), 200 shekels of silver (place the silver or gray silk into the bag), and a wedge of gold of 50 shekels weight (place the yellow or gold silk in the bag). Proceed to tell of the defeat and humiliation of Joshua and the people of Israel in battle.

Finally, relate how God told Joshua to stop crying about his defeat and get up off his knees and go out and sanctify the people. Achan, who thought he had pulled a fast one on God, was found out and confessed his sin. Read Joshua 7:20. As you do, reach into the bag and pull out the large black silk and show it to the audience.

Go on from this point to relate how important a biblical truth is to be found in this story. You can't escape God! No sin is ever hid from His sight. We may fool others, and even think for a while we've been successful in fooling God, but our sin will ultimately find us out! But there is good news. If we will own up to our sin and confess it, God is gracious and full of mercy. He stands ready to forgive us because of the provisions He has made for us through the atoning work of Christ our Saviour. Here you might wish to elaborate on the plan of salvation.

12

HABITS CAN BE BROKEN

Text: Philippians 4:13

MATERIALS

A magical effect sold by all magic dealers under the name of
Clippo
A pair of sharp scissors

EFFECT

Performer shows a strip of newspaper which may be handed
out for examination by the audience. The paper is first cut
straight through, and the performer shows the audience that he
has two separate pieces of paper which cannot be restored. Next
he folds one piece of paper in the center, as in figure 13*a,* and a
piece is cut off at that point with a pair of scissors. The cut-off
piece falls to the floor. The performer places the two pieces in

A

B

Fig. 13. How to use Clippo

44

the right hand, holding the end of one of the pieces between his index finger and thumb (see fig. 13b). The balance of the paper is now allowed to drop. To the amazement of the audience the paper has been restored into one complete strip.

MESSAGE

Talk on the subject of habits and how binding they can become in one's life, that when they are formed, they are extremely difficult to get rid of—or to cut out of—our lives. (This part of the message may vary, depending on which habits you wish to stress. You may wish to be general, or, with an older audience, you may wish to deal in specifics.)

Continue your message by exploring the idea that many people claim, "I can stop whenever I want to!" Such people feel that in their own strength they are the master of their life. (Here cut one of the pieces of newspaper straight through without the fold, as in fig. 13a. You will then have two pieces of paper which cannot be restored into a whole piece again.) Explain that if we try to break a habit in our own strength, we fail because most habits have such a grip on us that it takes a power outside of ourselves if we are to be successful.

However, if we attempt to cut out a habit in our lives, leaning in faith upon the strength and power of Jesus Christ, we will be victorious. (Here cut the second paper, as shown in fig. 13a and restore it to one "whole" piece as shown in fig. 13b.) Through Christ, our lives can be restored and made whole. We can be successful at "cutting out" the habits in our lives which are not pleasing to Christ our Saviour and Lord. Close by quoting Philippians 4:13, putting the emphasis on "through Christ which strengtheneth me."

13

LINKED LIVES

Text: Romans 14:7

MATERIALS

An 8-ounce glass (clear glass)
A piece of shiny metal or mirror glass
Six to ten small, solid metal rings
A chain of solid metal rings the same number and size as the
single rings
A large handkerchief

EFFECT

The single metal rings are shown separately and then dropped into the glass. The glass is covered with a handkerchief. When the handkerchief is removed from the glass and the rings are removed, they are now linked together, making a chain.

HOW TO PERFORM THE EFFECT

The metal or mirror is cut to the shape of the glass and is inserted in the center of the glass dividing it into two separate compartments (see fig. 14). The chain of linked metal rings is already in the rear compartment of the glass away from the audience. They cannot see the chain because of the metal or mirror partition. And, because of the partition, the glass appears to be empty. The glass is picked up with the right hand and placed in the palm of the left hand. (Be sure when you pick up the glass that you *do not* have any of your fingers toward the rear of the glass. Pick it up by the sides.) Drop the single metal rings, one by one, into the front compartment of the glass. Cover the glass with the handkerchief. As you are adjusting the handkerchief to completely cover the glass, turn the glass a half-turn. This will put the compartment with the linked metal rings toward the front and the compartment of the glass with the single metal rings toward the rear and away from the audience. Place the glass on the table. Remove the handkerchief from the glass. Reach into the glass and remove the chain of linked metal rings.

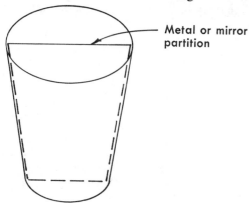

Fig. 14. The glass with two compartments

MESSAGE

Point out that the separate, single metal rings represent individual people. The glass represents the world in which we live. Develop the idea that many people have that as individuals what they do is their business. It will hurt only them and no one else. But this is *not true!* Our lives are linked to others through kinship, marriage, business, society, church, and so on. What we do, both the good things and the bad, does have an effect on others about us. Our lives are linked together with others.

Here you might wish to quote the text. As you develop the sermon, drop the individual metal rings into the glass. At the conclusion of the sermon, illustrate your point by removing the metal rings which are now formed into a chain, linking them together.

You may prefer to use various sizes and shapes of buttons; large ones, small ones, round ones, square ones, and so on. Each button could represent a certain type of person. Then when you remove them, they will be linked together on a piece of thread. If you use this suggestion, be sure that the same number, shape, color, and size buttons are strung on the thread as are used separately at the beginning of your sermon.

14

GOD'S LOVE FOR MAN

Text: Genesis 1 and 2; John 1:29; 3:16; 1 Corinthians 5:17

MATERIALS

A production box made of plywood (see figs. 15a and 15b)
A piece of mirror, cut to fit the production box
Spring flowers, birds, fish, fruit, snake (these can be secured
from any magic store or novelty shop)
A picture of Christ

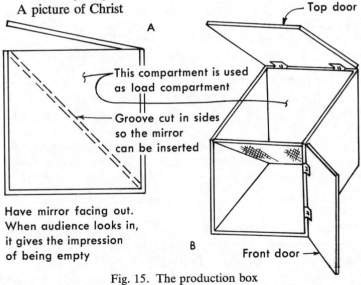

Top door

A

This compartment is used
as load compartment

Groove cut in sides
so the mirror
can be inserted

Have mirror facing out.
When audience looks in,
it gives the impression
of being empty

B

Front door →

Fig. 15. The production box

The production box should be made from ½ or ¾-inch plywood. A good size for the box is 10 inches square. The sides of the box should be grooved on the inside edge at a 45-degree angle. It should be approximately ¼-inch deep, and the width will depend on the thickness of the mirror to be used. Paint the outside of the box a bright, attractive color. Either paint the inside a bright color or use a colorful paper design. Make sure that the interior will show up in the mirror, giving the illusion of the box being empty when the front door is opened. Also be sure that the underside of the top door is painted or papered the same as the inside of the front compartment. The two doors should be hinged as in figure 15b.

EFFECT

The box is shown to the audience to be empty by opening the front door. The door is closed. The top door is opened, and items are produced from the box that a few moments before had been shown to be empty.

HOW TO PERFORM THE EFFECT

Place the items, in the order in which they are to be produced, in the rear compartment of the production box (see fig. 15a). The front door of the box is opened and left open long enough for the audience to get the illusion of the entire box being empty. Close the front door. Then at the right moment in your sermon, open the *top* door and produce the items from the box as needed to illustrate the message.

MESSAGE

Begin your sermon by showing that the box is empty. Tell the audience that the box represents the world before creation. Close the front door of the box and begin to relate the story of God's creation of the world. As you tell the story of the various phases of creation, open the top door of the box and produce the fruit, flowers, birds, fish, and so on. Then close the top door and tell the story of how sin came into the world and that because of sin, man's fellowship with God was ruined. Now open the top door and produce the snake from the box.

Continue by telling how Satan, disguised as a serpent, tempted Eve to disobey God by eating the forbidden fruit. She yielded to the temptation and in turn persuaded Adam to eat of the fruit also. Go into detail, using the passages from Genesis 1 and 2.

Close the top door to the box. Proceed to relate the story of God's love for mankind and plans for man's redemption. As you quote John 1:29 and 3:16, open the top door to the box, reach in, and take out the picture of Christ. Tell of God sending His Son to die in our behalf. Here relate the story of God's redemptive plan. Conclude your message by emphasizing 2 Corinthians 5:17-21.

15

THE REWARD OF CROSS-BEARING

Text: Matthew 16:24; Revelation 2:10

MATERIALS

A ½-yard of opaque, black (preferably felt) material
A ¼-yard of red material
A ¼-yard of white material

CONSTRUCTION DATA

Cut the black material in half, making two squares of cloth 18 inch × 18 inch (see fig. 16a). Hem one of the pieces on all four edges. Out of the other piece of black material, cut a flap large enough to be hemmed on three sides and sewn across the middle of the 18 inch × 18 inch piece of material (see fig. 16b). Cut a cross out of the red material, approximately 7 inches tall and the crossbar 4 inches in length. The cross should be 1 inch wide (see fig. 16c). Cut a crown out of the white material, 8 inches wide and 3 inches in depth (see fig. 16b). Sew the cross to the bottom half of the 18 inch × 18 inch material (see fig. 16c) and the crown to the flap (see fig. 16b).

EFFECT

The piece of black material with the red cross showing is shown to the audience. At the proper moment shake the cloth gently, and the cross mysteriously changes to a crown.

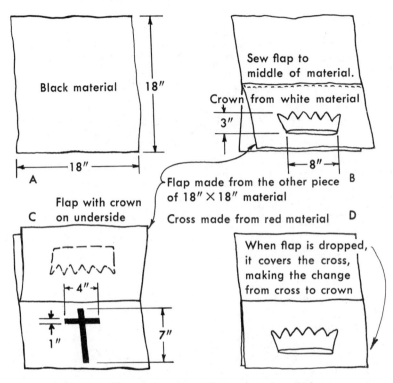

Fig. 16. The construction of the changing cloth

How to Perform the Effect

Hold the flap between your index fingers and thumbs against the top of the 18 inch × 18 inch material (see fig. 16c). Gently shake the cloth and at the same moment, let loose of the flap. The flap will drop and instantly cover the cross, creating the illusion that the cross has become a crown. Practice this before a mirror until you have the correct amount of motion to the cloth to cover the dropping of the flap. The motion of the cloth, if done properly, completely covers the dropping of the flap and creates a beautiful illusion.

Begin your message by quoting Matthew 16:24. Speak on the importance of cross-bearing in the life of a Christian. Stress the importance of denying oneself, bearing one's cross, and truly following in the footsteps of the Master. After you have completed this part of your message, point out the rewards that will be ours if we are truly faithful to Christ. You will find many passages of Scripture to use in reference to cross-bearing and the crown of life that we will receive as a reward for our faithfulness (e.g., Mt 10:38; 1 Co 9:24-27; Gal 6:14; Phil 4:1; 2 Ti 4:8; Heb 12:1-2; Ja 1:12; 1 Pe 5:4).

When you begin to talk on the crown of life, at this point, allow the flap to drop, mysteriously changing the cross to a crown. This illusion will drive home the point you are making.

16

MADE WHOLE THROUGH FAITH

Text: Mark 5:25-34

MATERIALS

 2 average size paper bags
 2 strings of Pop-It beads (the beads can be secured at a department store)

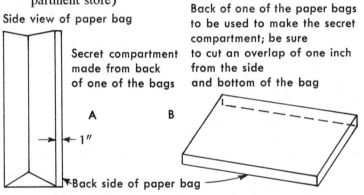

Side view of paper bag

Secret compartment made from back of one of the bags

Back of one of the paper bags to be used to make the secret compartment; be sure to cut an overlap of one inch from the side and bottom of the bag

A   B

1″

Back side of paper bag

Fig. 17. Bag with secret compartment

CONSTRUCTION DATA

Take two paper bags the same size, cut the back and at least one inch of the sides and bottom from one of them (see fig. 17*b*). Glue this section onto the back of the other paper bag, forming a secret compartment (see fig. 17*a*). Glue it along the sides and bottom, leaving the top open.

55

A string of beads is shown. It is snapped apart in four or five separate strands. The beads are then placed in the paper bag. The bag is then held by its sides with both hands and swung upward. The beads fly out of the bag into the air, having been restored into one strand of beads.

How to Perform the Effect

The paper bag with the secret compartment is on the table. One set of beads is in the bottom of the main part of the bag. Show the second set of beads and break them apart into four or five strands. Pick up the paper bag and drop these loose sections into the secret compartment on the back of the bag. Hold the secret compartment closed against the paper bag with the thumb and index finger of the left hand. In your right hand, hold the opposite side of the bag and give an upward flip to the bag. This will send the string of beads from the bottom of the main part of the paper bag into the air. The thumbs and first fingers of the hands are holding the secret compartment closed so that there is no fear of the loose beads falling out.

Message

The message can be based on the whole passage in Ephesians 4:13-16. Speak about how easy it is for one's life to become very fragmented. There is no wholeness to it. Here you would take the string of beads and break them into four or five strands. Then go on to tell how important faith is in one's life, that through faith in Jesus Christ, one's life can be made whole. Here, flip the bag and allow the string of beads to fly into the air, illustrating how one's life can be restored and made whole through faith in Christ Jesus our Saviour and Lord. After speaking about the lack of wholeness in one's life, you might wish to spend time to explain the plan of salvation. This message should have a lot of Scripture in it. As you prepare your message, always include as much Scripture and illustrations from the Bible as possible.

17

GATHERED TOGETHER IN CHRIST

Text: 2 Thessalonians 2:1

MATERIALS

Same as in chap. 16

EFFECT

A string of large, colored Pop-It beads is displayed and then held over the paper bag and taken apart one bead at a time and dropped into the bag. Suddenly the bag is flipped with an upward swing, and the string of beads flies into the air fully restored into one strand of beads.

HOW TO PERFORM THE EFFECT

Check Sermon in Magic No. 14. The same procedure is followed in performing this magic effect as in chapter 16, "Made Whole Through Faith." The only difference is that instead of breaking the Pop-It beads into only four or five strands, in this effect take the beads apart one by one.

MESSAGE

Begin by telling your audience that as you pop the beads from each other, they are naturally separated from one another as they are dropped separately into the paper bag. Continue by explaining that as Christians, when we die we are separated, the dead from the living and one from another, as we are buried in different parts of the world. However, the time will come when we will all be gathered together again.

Go on to explain that someday, in the framework of God's perfect plan, Jesus Christ will return. When He comes again, all Christians, both living and dead, will be caught up to meet the Lord in the air. The dead will be raised and the living changed and all together will be gathered to meet their Lord. (Here throw the restored beads from the bag to illustrate your point.)

18

THREE IN ONE

Text: 1 John 5:8

MATERIALS

A piece of construction paper 8 inches wide and 18 inches
  long

A cardboard cylinder approximately 1½ inches in diameter
  and 2½ inches in length (either paint the cylinder the same
  color as the construction paper or cover with a piece of the
  construction paper)

A small piece of red ribbon, ¾ inch wide

Three small silk handkerchiefs, one red, one white, and one
  blue

1 large silk with red, white, and blue colors blended

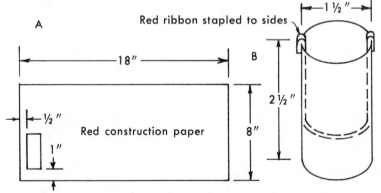

Fig. 18. The construction of the two cylinders

Construction Data

Glue and staple the cardboard cylinder to the top edge of the construction paper toward the left edge of the paper (see fig. 18*a*). Attach, by stapling, the ribbon across the top of the cardboard cylinder. Be sure that the ribbon is long enough to go about ⅔ the way down inside the cylinder (see fig. 18*b*).

Effect

Three different colored silks are shown separately along with a piece of construction paper. The construction paper is rolled into a cylinder. The three silks are placed one at a time into the cylinder. A moment later, when they are removed from the other end of the cylinder, they seem to have blended themselves together into one large silk with all the colors together.

How to Perform the Effect

The piece of construction paper should be laying on top of the table with the attached cardboard cylinder facing the table toward the performer and away from the audience (see fig. 19*a*). The large silk is already inside the cardboard cylinder (see fig. 19*b*).

To pick up the construction paper, reach under it with the right hand. Cup your hand over the cardboard cylinder, completely covering it with your hand. Now the piece of paper can be shown to the audience. Flip it over so that they can see both sides.

After showing both sides of the paper, roll it into a small cylinder with the secret cardboard cylinder on the inside (see fig. 19*b*). Now, one by one, place the small silk handkerchiefs into the paper cylinder. Be sure that they are crammed down inside the secret cardboard compartment. As they are pushed into the secret compartment, they will automatically push the large silk out of the secret compartment into the lower section of the paper cylinder. You do not have to worry about the three small silks,

60

as the ribbon will stop them from going all the way through the secret compartment.

Now all you need to do is wait for the right moment in your sermon to pull the large silk out of the paper cylinder. Again you will be able to show the construction paper to your audience as being empty. Be sure as you unroll the paper, that your hand is once again covering the secret cardboard cylinder. Practice covering the cylinder with your hand in front of a mirror. This way you'll be sure that you are holding it correctly.

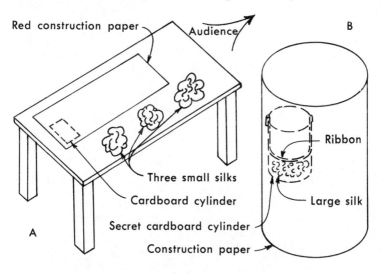

Fig. 19. The operation of the cylinders

MESSAGE

Draw attention to the text, 1 John 5:8. Point out that there are three things mentioned in the text, the Spirit, the water, and the blood. Enlarge upon this text by elaborating on the entire passage, verses 6 through 12. It is these three who bear witness to the truth. They bear witness that God has given to us, through Christ, eternal life.

Continue by stating that, according to John, these three witnesses agree and are one. Let the blue silk represent the Spirit, the white silk the water, and the red silk the blood. As you say this, place them in the paper cylinder one at a time.

Talk about the agreement of these witnesses and how they are one in their testimony. Reach into the cylinder and pull out the large silk and show the audience that the three silks have now become blended together into one. There is unity in the testimony of God. These three agree as one and bear witness.

19

MADE RIGHT THROUGH FAITH

Text: Acts 8:14-24

MATERIALS

A gilt-edged picture frame, size 5 inches by 7 inches
A thin sheet of colored paper
A small piece of taffeta or rayon material of matching color
A dark, colorful handkerchief approximately 24 inches square
A thin sheet of white paper
A small piece of red taffeta or rayon material

CONSTRUCTION DATA

The frame must consist of three simple parts: (1) the frame, which must have slotted sides and one partly opened end; (2) the glass, which slides into the grooves and which must drop to the front of the frame; (3) a cardboard backing, which goes into the groove and holds the glass in place. Such a frame can be purchased from any dime store. After you have secured the proper frame, take out the inside backing and cover it with a dark black paper. Use paper long enough so the ends can be carried over the top, bottom, and sides, forming a narrow band on the outside of the backing. Glue the paper firmly in place.

Next, cut out a large white heart from the piece of paper and glue it to the center of the cardboard backing (see fig. 20a).

Next cut the piece of fabric to the exact width of the cardboard backing but one inch longer so it can be carried over the top edge and a little way down the outside of the back (see fig. 20b). Now

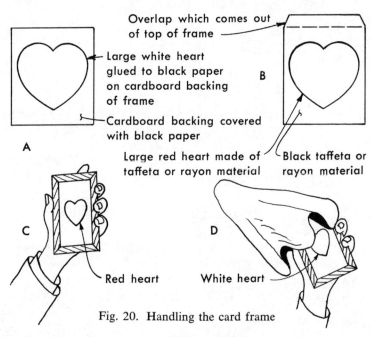

Overlap which comes out of top of frame

Large white heart glued to black paper on cardboard backing of frame

B

Cardboard backing covered with black paper

A

Large red heart made of taffeta or rayon material

Black taffeta or rayon material

C

D

Red heart

White heart

Fig. 20. Handling the card frame

cut a large heart from the red fabric and either glue or sew with red thread to the large piece of black fabric.

To prepare the frame, slide the glass into the frame. Hold the frame with the glass downward and slide the cloth fabric with the red heart attached into the frame. Now slide the cardboard backing with the white heart attached into the frame. Be sure that the inch of the fabric protrudes at the top through the open end of the frame. Bend the fabric over the back and work the edges firmly beneath the back portion of the frame.

EFFECT

A picture frame is shown with black background and large red heart. It is then covered with a large handkerchief. When the handkerchief is removed, the red heart has now been transformed into a white heart.

64

Hold the frame upright in the left hand, its front toward the audience, showing the picture of the red heart (see fig. 20*c*). The black fabric under the glass will look like the black backing when the white heart is revealed.

Cover the frame with the large handkerchief. Now, gripping the handkerchief above the frame with the right thumb and fingers, grasp the projecting fabric, working it into the folds of the handkerchief. When the handkerchief is pulled away, the piece of fabric comes with it, revealing the cardboard backing with the white heart on it (see fig. 20*d*). The frame may now be handed out for examination if you so wish. The piece of fabric is laid aside with the handkerchief.

MESSAGE

Begin by reading the passage of Scripture from Acts 8. Then explain how important it is to have the right motive in wanting to serve Christ. Our service, if it is to be genuine and acceptable to God, must stem from a deep inner desire to serve Him and to bring others to a saving knowledge of Jesus Christ as Saviour and Lord. We should never seek to elevate ourselves as a result of any talents or gifts God may have bestowed upon us.

Simon wanted the gift of the laying on of hands upon others so that they might receive the Holy Spirit. He wanted to buy the gift rather than pay the price of self-dedication and discipline. His motive was entirely selfish. He was interested in promoting and elevating *Simon,* not Christ or the Holy Spirit. Peter rebuked him by saying that his problem was that his heart was not right with God.

The requirement for true discipleship is a heart that is right with God. And the only way we can have a right standing with God is through faith in Jesus Christ. At this point in your sermon you should go into detail explaining what faith in Christ means. Point out that, through submission to the will of God through Christ, our hearts can be changed and our lives made right with God. You might wish to refer to Ephesians 2:8-9 or other similar passages of Scripture.

To conclude your sermon, you will drive home your point by showing the frame with the picture of the red heart in it, which represents our hearts when they are not right with God (Ro 6: 20-23). Then, as you quote Isaiah 1:18, remove the handkerchief from the frame and reveal the picture of the white heart. This will demonstrate that through faith in Christ our hearts are changed, and, as a result, our lives are transformed. Made right through faith, we are now new creatures in Christ Jesus.

This same effect can be used to simply explain the plan of salvation, using Isaiah 1:18 as your text. You will also find other wonderful uses for the card frame: It's a great effect! Use your imagination and you'll be surprised at some of the ideas that will come to you.

20

STARS THAT TRULY SHINE

Text: Daniel 12:3

MATERIALS

A Thumb Tip, a magical accessory sold by all magic dealers at a very reasonable price, will lend itself to many magical effects

A box of small gold stars

EFFECT

Show your hands to be empty. Close your left hand; reach over with your right hand as if you are clutching the left. When you remove the right hand, slowly turn the left hand over and let the gold stars drift from your closed hand to the floor.

HOW TO PERFORM THE EFFECT

Place as many gold stars in the bottom of the thumb tip as you can and still be able to put it comfortably on the tip of your right thumb. Don't worry about it being seen. Your audience does not expect it to be there, and, as it is flesh colored, it will blend into your hand. When you show your hands to the audience, don't look at your thumb. Just look at the audience and slowly turn your hands, showing them both sides.

Then close your left hand into a fist. Reach over with your right hand and clasp your left hand. As you do this, let your right thumb—with the tip on it—go inside your left fist. Deposit the Thumb Tip in your left hand. Remove your right hand.

At the right moment, slowly turn your left fist over with thumb and index finger toward the floor. Empty the gold stars from the tip onto the floor. As the last stars are still falling to the floor, nonchalantly put your left hand in your pocket, leaving the thumb tip there. You can now again show both hands to be empty. If you do this before a mirror until you develop natural moves, you will see how effective this accessory can be.

MESSAGE

Show your hands to your audience and begin by saying, "As you can see my hands are empty." Then proceed to tell them that there are many Christians, who, because they have failed to be the faithful witnesses for Christ that they should have been, will one day stand in His presence empty handed. You might want to quote or sing the song, "Must I Go and Empty Handed?" at this point. Continue by explaining how tragic this will be. Such a person will be much like the person in the parable Jesus told who hid his talent in the earth (Mt 25).

We do not need to go into the presence of our Lord empty handed. All we need to do is be faithful in our work and witness for Christ. At this point quote Daniel 12:3, and as you finish it simply close by saying to them, "Instead of going empty handed, let us go this way." Slowly let the gold stars drift to the floor. Conclude by saying, "And those of us who have been busy about our Father's business of winning souls for Him shall shine like the stars for ever and ever. In so doing, not only will we find life in all of its abundance here in this life, but in glorifying God through our lives, we add stars to our crown which someday we shall receive from Him who loved us and gave Himself for us."

21

REMEMBER THEIR SINS NO MORE

Text: Hebrews 8:12

MATERIALS

A piece of cloth, 9 inches wide and 27 inches long
A wooden egg or any small object

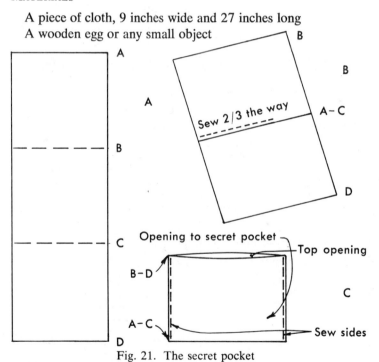

Fig. 21. The secret pocket

Fold the cloth at B (see fig. 21a) and sew it two-thirds of the way across at point C (see fig. 21b); then fold D across to meet end B and sew up both sides of the bag (see fig. 21c). This will form a secret pocket at the bottom of the bag.

EFFECT

The bag is shown to be just an ordinary bag by showing both the outside and inside of the bag to the audience. The egg is then placed in the bag. The audience is again shown the bag by inverting it to show that the egg has disappeared.

HOW TO PERFORM THE EFFECT

Be sure the side of the bag that has the secret compartment is toward you. Hold the bag with the left hand. Show that the egg or object is solid by hitting it on the top of the table. Place it in the bag with the right hand. Be sure that you tuck it safely into the hole of the secret compartment. Tip the bag slightly so that the egg can roll down into the corner of the secret compartment that is sewed (see fig. 22a). When the bag is turned upside down, the egg will automatically fall to the top of the compartment. It can now be safely inverted to show that the egg has disappeared (see fig. 22b).

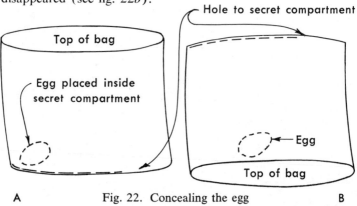

A   Fig. 22. Concealing the egg   B

MESSAGE

State that you would like to illustrate your text by using an egg and a cloth bag. The egg will represent sin, and the bag will represent the atoning work of Jesus Christ on the cross. At this point in your message, drive home the importance of having one's sins forgiven and how this is only possible through faith in Jesus Christ and His atoning work in our behalf. (You may wish to use such passages of Scripture as Jn 1:29; Ro 5:9; 5:12; 5:20; 6:10; 6:23; 2 Co 5:21; Eph 1:7; 2:13; Col 1:14; Heb 9:22; 1 Jn 1:7-8; 2:1; Rev 1:5.)

After you have developed your sermon, then to illustrate your major point—that if our sins are truly forgiven through repentance and faith, then God truly forgives and remembers them no more—take the bag and egg and illustrate the point by making the egg, which represents sin, disappear.

After you have made this type bag, you will find many ways in which it can be used to illustrate spiritual truths. One suggestion to develop is the use of the text, "Be sure your sin will find you out" (Num 32:23). Tell the story of a little boy thinking that he can steal and not be caught. He hides the toy he stole but to his amazement his parents find it. Use a small toy which will fit the bag. Make it disappear and show the bag empty. Then reach in and pull it out again. This will give you some idea of how versatile this magical effect is. Just be creative, and you'll be amazed how many ideas will come to you once you have mastered this effect.

22

GROWING IN GRACE

Text: 2 Peter 3:18

MATERIALS

A piece of soft rope 48 inches long
A small rubber band

EFFECT

The performer takes a short piece of rope from his coat pocket. He casually shows it to the audience and then proceeds to visibly stretch the rope making it 3 times its original length.

HOW TO PERFORM THE EFFECT

The rope must be prepared beforehand, as shown in figure 23a. It is then held, as shown in figure 23b, with the coil of rope concealed in the palm of the right hand.

To perform the effect, have the rope in your right coat pocket. Reach in with the right hand and grasp the rope making sure that the coil of rope is completely concealed in the palm of the right hand before removing it from the pocket. Bring the rope out of the pocket and casually show it to the audience. If your motions are natural and casual, your audience will not suspect that there is a coil of rope in the palm of your right hand. *Do not* look down at your right hand. This will only draw attention to it.

At the right moment, grasp the end of the rope with the left hand and slowly stretch the rope. When you have completed the effect, you can throw the rope to your audience so that they can examine it.

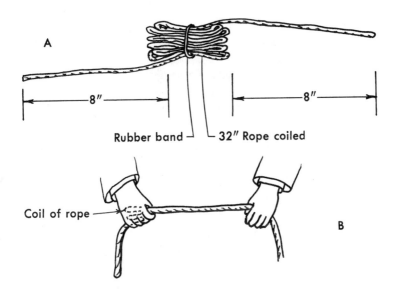

Fig. 23. The rope that stretches

Begin your message by pointing out how important it is to grow to spiritual maturity, that Christ is vitally concerned that we not remain as babes spiritually. (You may wish to use such passages of Scripture as 1 Co 3:1-3; Eph 4:7; 11-15; 1 Th 1:3; 1 Pe 2:2 to develop your sermon.)

Continue by saying that the short piece of rope which you hold in your hand represents the life of one who has only recently accepted Christ as his Lord and Saviour, a young babe in Christ. Then quote 2 Peter 3:18, which tells us that we are not to remain as babes in Christ, but we are to keep on growing in grace and in the knowledge of our Lord and Saviour. As we daily read our Bible, study and meditate upon it, pray and seek to find His will for our lives, and then go forth to serve Him, we will grow in our spiritual lives, even as the piece of rope you hold keeps getting longer and longer.

Conclude by pointing out that as we grow in grace and knowledge, we become more useful to God and to others, even as this longer piece of rope is of more use than a short piece.

This is a tremendously effective magic object lesson to drive home this important spiritual truth. Do not underestimate its effectiveness because of the apparent simplicity of it.

23

THE SUBTLETY OF SIN

Text: Romans 6:12-14

MATERIALS

A gilt-edged picture frame, 5 inches by 7 inches
A sheet of black paper
A small piece of taffeta or rayon material of matching color
A dark, colorful handkerchief approximately 24 inches square
Three balls of thin wool thread, one red, one blue, and one gold
A base to hold the frame

CONSTRUCTION DATA

The frame that is to be used in this effect must be identical to the one used in chapter 19, "Made Right Through Faith." Refer back to this sermon for more information.

Take the cardboard backing out of the frame and cover it with black paper. Use a large enough piece of paper so that the ends can be carried over the top, bottom, and sides, forming a narrow band on the outside of the backing. Glue the paper firmly in place.

Now take a thin-tip, gold felt marker and draw a spider's web with a large spider in the center of it, as shown in figure 24a.

Next cut the piece of taffeta or rayon material to the exact width of the cardboard backing, but make it one inch longer than the backing, so that it can be carried over the top edge (see fig. 24b).

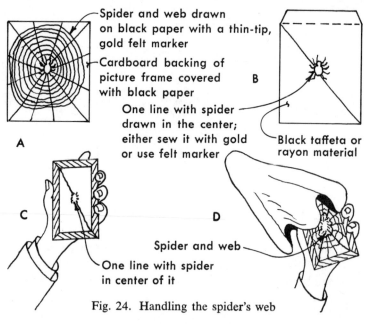

Spider and web drawn on black paper with a thin-tip, gold felt marker

Cardboard backing of picture frame covered with black paper

One line with spider drawn in the center; either sew it with gold or use felt marker

A

B

Black taffeta or rayon material

C

D

Spider and web

One line with spider in center of it

Fig. 24. Handling the spider's web

Now either sew a single line across the fabric with gold thread and a spider in the center, or use the gold felt marker and draw it on the fabric. Prepare the frame for this effect in the same manner described in chapter 19.

EFFECT

A picture frame is shown with black background, and a spider is in the center of it, attached to one thin web. A large handkerchief is then placed over it, and it is placed in the base (see fig. 25). Then several different colored balls of wool thread are shown and one is selected by the audience. The ball selected is placed under the handkerchief. When the handkerchief is removed, there in the frame is the colored spider's web, with the spider sitting in the middle of it. The web which has been spun by the spider is the same color as the ball of wool thread chosen by the audience.

Hold the picture frame upright in the left hand, its front toward the audience showing them the picture of the spider in the center of the single thread (see fig. 24c). The fabric beneath the glass will look like the backing when the spider in the center of the web is revealed.

Cover the frame with the large handkerchief.

Now, gripping the handkerchief above the frame with the right thumb and fingers, grasp the projecting fabric, which has been tucked into the sides of the frame at the back. Work the fabric into the folds of the handkerchief. When the handkerchief is pulled away, the piece of fabric will come with it, revealing the cardboard backing with the picture of the spider and her web (see fig. 24d). The frame may now be handed out for examination if you wish. The piece of fabric is laid aside with the handkerchief.

Here is how to assure that the gold thread is chosen. Place the three balls of colored wool thread on the table. Ask someone in the audience to please choose any two of the colors for you and call them out. Place these two balls of thread to one side. If he happens to choose the blue and red ball, you merely thank the person and say that the gold is the color which has been freely chosen. If, on the other hand, he happens to choose either the blue and gold or red and gold, then place them aside separate from the one not chosen. Now ask someone else to please choose one of these colors and call it out. If they choose the blue, you merely say, "Thank you, that now leaves us with the gold thread left out of the three colors which you had to choose from." If, on the other hand, the gold ball is selected, thank the person and say, "As you can see, the gold ball has been freely chosen by the audience from the three colors they were given to select from." No matter what colors they choose, with this technique, you will always come up with the color that is already in the picture which will be revealed.

You will find many uses for this type of choice of any three objects. It is simple yet very convincing.

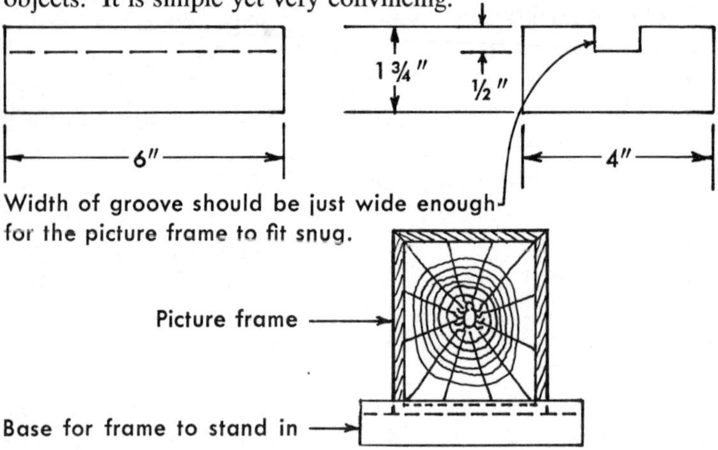

Width of groove should be just wide enough for the picture frame to fit snug.

Picture frame ⟶

Base for frame to stand in ⟶

Fig. 25. Construction of the base

MESSAGE

Begin your sermon by referring to Genesis 3 and tell the story of the Fall of man. Point out how subtle Satan really is and how easy it is to be taken in by him. Talk about how really deadly sin can be in our lives and also the tragic consequences of sin.

Continue your sermon by stating that the subtlety of Satan is much like a spider weaving her web. The purpose of the web is to catch unwary insects so that she might devour them. The threads in the web woven by Satan are sins. (Now show the picture frame with the spider on just a single thin thread. She looks so harmless and even attractive.) Continue by saying that the spider likes to build her web in dark and out-of-the-way places. In this manner, she can more easily entrap insects. Then cover the frame with the handkerchief for a few moments. Then point out that the three balls of yarn represent sin and its attractiveness. Ask the question, "What is your weakness and sin? Maybe you'd rather not tell, because usually these are things we attempt to keep a secret." Then ask someone to stand, and, by using the method explained, have the person choose a ball of thread. After the gold ball of yarn has been selected, place it under the handkerchief.

Continue your sermon by stating that when the handkerchief is removed, they will be able to see how mysteriously sin can spin a web about us, and, before we know it, Satan has entrapped us. (Remove the handkerchief and show your audience how the spider has mysteriously woven a web from the gold yarn that had been selected.)

You may now point out that this is the way it is with temptation. If we continue to yield to it, before long, we have become trapped by it.

Refer to the text and tell how we can be successful over temptation and sin, subtle as it may be, by simply accepting the gift of salvation freely given to us by God through the atoning work of Jesus Christ on Calvary in our behalf. Emphasize the gift of grace. Point out that the secret to victorious Christian living is to be found in the thirteenth verse: "Do not go on presenting the members of your body to sin as instruments of unrighteousness; but present yourselves to God . . . as instruments of righteousness to God" (NASB).

24

BEING MADE WHOLE

Text: John 5:1-15

MATERIALS

A piece of soft rope approximately 5 feet long (*do not* use rope that has a plastic film or covering on it; the rope must be very pliable)

A pair of scissors

EFFECT

A piece of rope is shown to the audience and then is cut into two pieces by a spectator. The two pieces are then knotted and shown as two pieces of rope which have been tied together. The rope is then coiled around the performer's left hand. When it is uncoiled, it is shown to have been restored into one piece again. The rope may then be thrown to audience for their examination.

HOW TO PERFORM THE EFFECT

Hold the rope as in figure 26a, between the left thumb and left index finger and the index finger of the right hand through the loop of the rope. Now lift the loop with the right hand and raise it to the point marked X as in figure 26a. This point on the rope should be approximately one half-inch below the little finger of the left hand. At this point the forefinger and thumb of the right hand should grasp the rope and pull it through the loop (see fig. 26b). Now let the loop slide off the right finger and bring it up even with the two ends, thereby forming a new loop

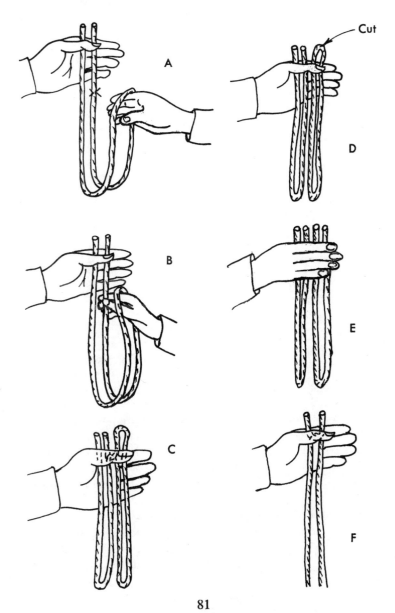

A

Cut

D

B

E

C

F

81

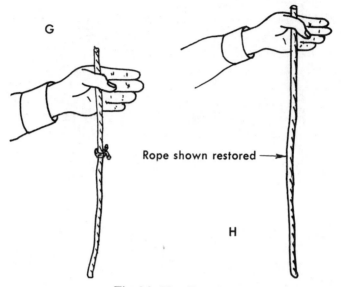

Fig. 26. Handling the rope

(see fig. 26c). Do not worry about the fake loop; the thumb and fingers of the left hand will hide the fake loop as in figure 26d. (Be sure that the fingers of the left hand are at all times facing the audience.) The fake loop is then cut by the spectator (see fig. 26d).

From the audience's point of view, there are now four ends of rope appearing above the fingers of the left hand (see fig. 26e). The two center pieces of rope are held by the thumb and fingers and each of the outside pieces is removed by the right hand and allowed to fall free causing it to appear to the audience as two pieces of rope (see fig. 26f).

The two ends protruding above the hand are now tied into a knot and the ends of the knot trimmed to facilitate getting rid of the fake knot. The rope is then held at the extreme end, hanging down, and attention is drawn to the fact that two short pieces of rope are now tied by a knot at the center (see fig. 26g).

The rope is then wrapped around the left hand. As this is being done, the right hand secretly slides off the fake knot. With the fake knot palmed in the right hand, reach into the right coat pocket and take out a wand or some other object to be used to make the knot disappear and the rope restored into one piece again. As you do this, simply drop the fake knot into the pocket. Hand the wand to the spectator who cut the rope and ask him or her to wave it over the rope, which is still coiled around your hand. Then slowly uncoil the rope and show the audience that it is now in one piece again. (Practice this effect before a mirror until you have developed confidence in forming the fake loop with one casual motion of the right hand. Be *sure* that you *do not* look down at your hands while you are forming the fake loop. This will only draw the attention of the audience to your hands.)

MESSAGE

Tell the story of the man who had been sick for thirty-eight years, as recorded in the text. This man had tried to find healing at the pool of Bethesda but had been unsuccessful. One day Jesus came along and asked him if he really would like to be healed—or made whole—again. Jesus then ordered him to get up off his pallet, pick it up, and walk away. To the astonishment of the lame man and everyone else present, he did just that. He, through faith, had been made whole.

After telling the story, go on to tell that this is a wonderful illustration of what sin can do in one's life. Before mankind was infected with the dread disease of sin, man had been created whole in the sight of God. (Now here is where you use the restored rope effect to illustrate your sermon. Let the rope represent man in his condition of wholeness in the sight of God.) You then explain that by cutting the rope you would like to illustrate the power of sin to sever the divine pattern God had in mind for man when He created him in His own image. As a result of sin, the Bible declares that all of us have sinned and thus have fallen short of the glory or divine image of God. Therefore, God sent His Son to rescue us and bring us back into a right relationship with the Father. Jesus died in our behalf on Calvary. Today Jesus comes to us, as He did to this man in our story, and asks us the important question with regard to the disease of sin in our souls: "Would you really like to be whole?" If we answer yes and yield to His plan of salvation so freely given, we can be made whole, even as the rope is now made whole again.

This is a wonderful effect to drive home the truth that if anyone, in simple faith, will accept Jesus Christ as his Lord and Saviour, his life can be made whole and he can live life in all of its abundance.

25

THE MIGHTY POWER OF THE CROSS

Text: 1 Corinthians 1:17

MATERIALS

Two pieces of soft rope 12 feet long
Five large curtain rings
A man's coat
A high-back chair

EFFECT

Two pieces of rope are shown to the audience. The five curtain rings are strung onto the ropes and tied with a single knot, as in figure 27a. Two ends of the rope are then threaded through the sleeve of the coat and held by one of the volunteers. The other two ends of the rope are threaded through the other sleeve of the coat and held by the second volunteer. The coat is then draped over the back of the chair (see fig. 27b). Have each of the volunteers hand you one end of the rope that he is holding, and another knot is tied on the outside of the coat, as in figure 27c. The volunteers are then asked to pull on the ropes. The rings and coat will come free while the ropes will be stretched out straight between the volunteers.

HOW TO PERFORM THE EFFECT

The pieces of rope are tied with thread, as in figure 27e. Fold the ropes back, as in figure 27f, and hold them so as to conceal the loop from the audience. Thread the ends of the rope into the

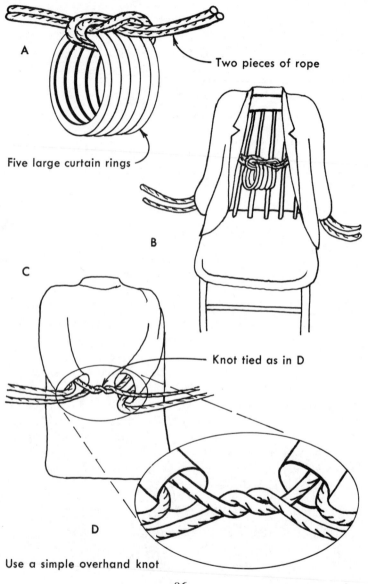

A

Two pieces of rope

Five large curtain rings

B

C

Knot tied as in D

D

Use a simple overhand knot

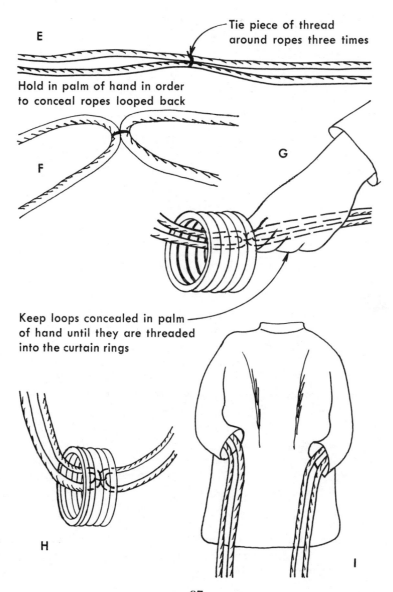

E Tie piece of thread around ropes three times

Hold in palm of hand in order to conceal ropes looped back

F

G

Keep loops concealed in palm of hand until they are threaded into the curtain rings

H

I

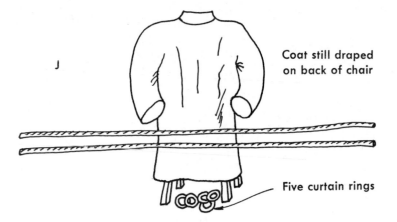

J

Coat still draped
on back of chair

Five curtain rings

Fig. 27. The operation of the rope and rings

five curtain rings, as in figure 27g. Be sure to keep the secret joint concealed in the palm of your hand until it is inside of the five curtain rings as in figure 27h.

The ropes are then tied around the curtain rings with a single knot (see fig. 27a). Two ends of the rope are threaded through the sleeve of the coat and held by one volunteer. The other two ends are threaded through the other sleeve and held by the other volunteer. The coat is then placed over the back of the chair, as in figure 27b. Figure 27b shows how the arrangement looks to you, and figure 27i shows it from the audience's point of view. Take a piece of rope from each volunteer and tie in one knot (see fig. 27d). Have the volunteers hold tightly to their ends of the ropes and pull. As they do, the five rings and the coat will fall off the ropes and the knots will disappear. The finish will appear as in figure 27j.

MESSAGE

Tell the story of the Fall of man in the Garden of Eden and how since then sin has had a tremendously binding effect on mankind. (Show the ropes and say that you are going to let them represent sin. Then show the curtain rings and coat and say that they will represent individuals who have sinned against God.) Here you might want to quote Romans 3:23 and 6:23.

As you are telling your audience about the binding effect of sin, thread the ropes through the rings, tying the knot around them. Then feed the ropes through the sleeves of the coat. Place it on the back of the chair and tie the loop in one rope. Give the ends of the ropes to the volunteers to hold.

Now relate the story of the cross of Christ and the redemptive work He accomplished there. Tell about the power of the cross to break the shackles of sin. Here you will want to quote and emphasize 1 Corinthians 1:18, that the preaching of the cross, the Gospel, is the power of God.

At this point have the assistants pull on the ropes and release the rings and the coat.

Then draw your conclusion. As the ropes are now released from the rings and the coat, so we can be immediately released from sin and its consequences through faith in Jesus Christ our Lord. Believe, accept, commit, and serve!

26

THE STRONG GRIP OF SIN

Text: Proverbs 5:22-23 (TLB)

MATERIALS

A dark glass bottle with a long neck (see fig. 28a)
A piece of rope ¼-inch thick and approximately 24 inches in
length
A small cork

CONSTRUCTION DATA

If you cannot find a suitable dark bottle, use any long-necked
bottle and paint it on the inside. The reason for the bottle being
prepared so that the audience cannot see the inside is the concealed cork, which is referred to in magic circles as a "gimmick"
(see fig. 28b). The cork should be shaped into a ball ¼ to ⅝
inches smaller than the neck of the bottle (see fig. 28c). This can
be done easily by the use of a single-edged razor blade.

EFFECT

A piece of rope is shown to the audience. It is then inserted
into the neck of the bottle. The bottle is then turned upside down
and the rope remains suspended in the bottle. The performer
then takes hold of the rope and the bottle is now shown to be
suspended by the rope. The rope is then taken out of the bottle,
and the bottle and rope are given to the audience for examination.

The cork is already in the bottom of the bottle before doing the effect. The audience is unaware of the cork "gimmick" inside the bottle. Show the bottle and the rope to the audience.

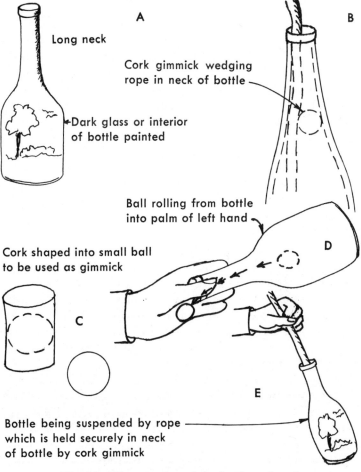

Fig. 28. The operation of the bottle and cork

At the right moment in your message, insert about 12 to 14 inches of the rope into the bottle. When the bottle is turned upside down, the cork will roll to the neck of the bottle. Gently pull on the rope and this will cause the cork to wedge the rope into the neck of the bottle (see fig. 28b). The rope can then be held and the bottle can be suspended in air by the rope.

At the conclusion of the effect, merely push the rope down into the neck of the bottle far enough to disengage the cork. Pull the rope out of the bottle with the right hand, holding the bottle by the neck with the left hand. Hand the rope to the audience for inspection. As you hand the rope to one of the spectators, slightly turn the bottle up and allow the cork to roll out into the palm of the left hand (see fig. 28d). Hand the bottle out for inspection with the right hand while palming the cork in the left.

MESSAGE

To illustrate your message, be sure that you explain at the outset that the bottle you hold will represent a person's life, and the rope will represent the habits and sins in our lives that take hold of us and bind us.

Start the message by quoting the text from Proverbs 5:22-23. Place the emphasis on verse 22, "They are ropes that catch and hold us" (TLB).

At this point elaborate on how easy it is to get caught in the snare of sin. So often we feel self-sufficient. We feel that we can do something, even though we know it is wrong, but that we will be the master of it. We'll do it just a few times and then quit. So often when people are confronted with something they are doing they'll quickly answer, "Well, it's not a habit, I can do it or leave it alone." Yet little do they know that each time they do it, it is becoming more binding upon them. If you wish, you can become more specific at this point by illustrating with such habits as smoking, drinking, gambling, lying, and so on. (Here you can illustrate that at first it does appear to be easy to give up by putting the rope in the bottle and pulling it out again.)

Then continue by pointing out that after a while, every sinful habit has a way of becoming the master of everyone who plays with sin. Little by little sin binds us and makes us its slave. (Here illustrate by putting the rope back into the bottle. As you talk about sin and enslavement to it, turn the bottle upside down so that the cork gimmick lodges in the neck of the bottle. Show how the rope is now suspended from the bottle and cannot be removed.) Continue by talking about how sin and habits get a grip on us and before long, we cannot free ourselves from them. In fact, they get such a strong grip that after a while our habits control us. (Illustrate your point now by showing how the rope is able to hold the bottle suspended in air. At this point, you may wish to quote such scripture passages as Ro 7:5-25; Gal 5:17; Eph 2:1; 2 Ti 2:26; Titus 3:3; 1 Jn 2:16; Rev 3:17.)

After you have driven home your message of how powerful sinful habits can be in one's life, conclude by telling them the Good News, that through the atoning work of Christ on Calvary, there is a way—in fact, the only way—whereby one can be released from the binding effect of sin. Here quote Romans 7:24-25. It is through Christ that we are delivered from sin and its consequences. Present to your audience the plan of salvation at this point. (Along with the very familiar passages of Scripture you may wish to use Ac 13:38-39; Col 2:13-14; 2 Ti 2:26; 1 Jn 1:7; 2:1-2; Re 1:5.) Here you can illustrate your point by releasing the bottle from the rope and handing them both out to your audience for inspection.

This is a great effect. Do not minimize its impact on an audience because of its simplicity.

This effect could be used to speak on any particular sin or habit rather than a general sermon. It would be great to point out the evils of drinking, lying, stealing, and so on. The more you work with effects such as this one, the more you will find creative uses for it.

PART III

PAPER TEARING

27

MAGIC WITH PAPER

IN THIS SECTION I would like to share with you some basic ideas in the use of newspapers and regular white paper in the art of paper-tearing and conjuring. One does not hear very much these days about this art. However, it can be a fascinating way of getting across certain truths from the Word of God. At the end of this chapter, I have given some starter ideas, but I do not go into detail as far as their application to specific illustrations or sermons, for I feel that as you learn the basic art of paper conjuring, you'll develop your own ideas for their use.

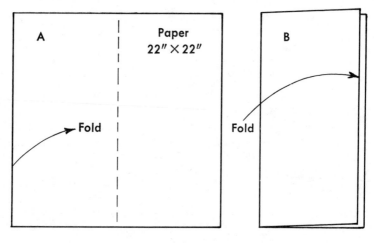

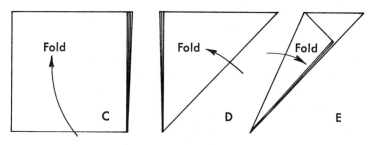

Figs. 29 a-e are the five basic folds for such paper tears as the ship's wheel and string of fish.

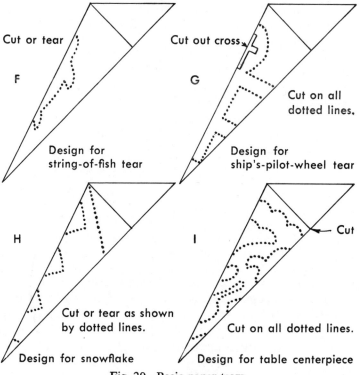

Fig. 29. Basic paper tears

Let's start with the basic folds needed in order to accomplish the paper tear for such unique designs as the ship's pilot wheel, a string of fish or dolls, a snowflake, and a table centerpiece. Any size paper can be used, but I prefer a piece of white paper 22 inches square. A nice type of paper that is easy to work with is blank, white newsprint. Be sure that prior to any paper-tearing, you have prefolded the paper. Then open it back out, so that, as far as your audience is concerned, you're starting from scratch. If you prefer to tear the design rather than use scissors, tear about an inch or so at a time instead of trying to give long tears. Don't be in a hurry. Always tear toward yourself.

Your paper-tearing will be seen best if you will have some type of dark backdrop to hold it in front of. A piece of dark cloth or even a blackboard will do.

The Paper Tree

Make a tube by rolling tightly a double piece of newspaper from one side to the other. When you are approximately 5 inches from the edge, add another double-page sheet (see fig. 30a). Keep on rolling; then add the third sheet in the same manner. Be sure to bring the paper toward you as you roll it. This will help keep the roll tight. Periodically tap the ends of the roll in order to keep them even.

Place a small rubber band around the center of the tube to hold it together. Then flatten half the tube. Now tear down the center of the flattened portion. In order to be sure that you tear a straight line, tear only about an inch at a time. When this is completed, then flatten the torn sheets together and tear down again. You will now have four torn parts. Each part will contain a lot of strips. Separate the four parts and bend the strips out from the tube (see fig. 30c). Now remove the rubber band from the tube.

Now put two fingers into the tube at the top, and, with your thumb, take hold of a couple of strips where they bend and pull them up gently. Do this slowly pulling only a few inches at a

96

time. After the strips are freely coming out of the tube, take your fingers out and work the tree upward from the outside.

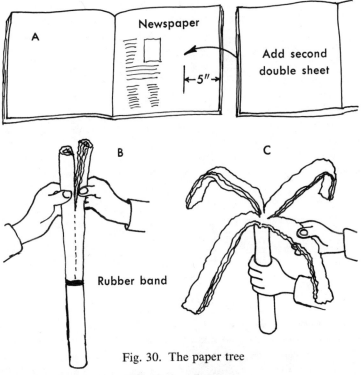

Fig. 30. The paper tree

THE PAPER LADDER

Make up a roll of newspaper just as you did for the paper tree. Flatten the tube so as to make it easier to work with. Then tear half through the tube twice, as shown in figure 31a. Please note the proportions of the tears. Next tear out the part between the first two tears, as shown in figure 31b.

The ends of the torn tube must now be bent down at right angles to the center part (see fig. 31c). Be careful at this point not to tear off any of the central strips.

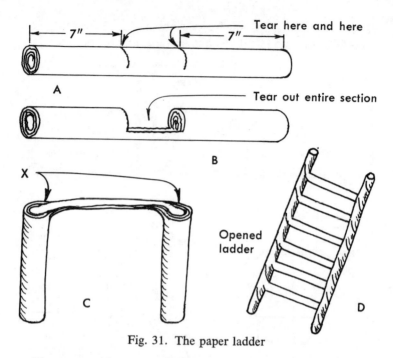

Fig. 31. The paper ladder

Now comes the more difficult move. It is now necessary to insert a finger in each tube at the Xs (see fig. 31c) and draw the ends upward, forming a beautiful ladder. Ask your assistant to hold the lower ends of the tube as you extend the ladder.

Small children especially love this effect. As the paper stretches upward, the ladder gradually takes on an amazing lifelike appearance. This is a beautiful effect to use when you are talking on the subject of Jacob's experience, as recorded in Genesis 28.

I might add that the length of the ladder will be determined by your skill and the length of the paper used. It is best, if you are experienced enough with handling paper magic, to use a number of pieces of double newspaper. If it is too hard to tear, then use a sharp knife to make the cuts. The larger it is the more impressive! Especially is this true when working with smaller children.

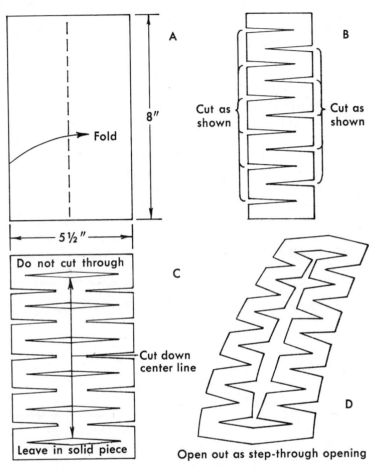

Fig. 32. The expanding paper card

THE EXPANDING PAPER CARD

Take a piece of regular typing paper and cut it down to five-and one-half inches by eight inches. With this small piece of paper, you can perform a magical effect that really has a tremendous punch.

Show your audience this small piece of paper. Then ask the question, "Do you think it is possible for me to step through this paper with my entire body?" Of course the answer will be no. For it appears to be totally impossible. Then proceed to show them how it is possible through the ability to cut it properly.

When doing this particular effect, it is best to use a sharp pair of scissors to achieve the proper effect. As you use this effect, you will find that it has many applications. The only drawback is that it should *never* be used the second time before the same audience. If so, you will lose the impact of the effect.

I think that the illustrations in figure 32 are self-explanatory. One warning: be sure to do this effect a few times in private before you use it before an audience. It is important that you make the cuts on both sides of the paper no deeper than 2 inches. If they are made too deep, the paper will tear at the weakest point and ruin the effect.

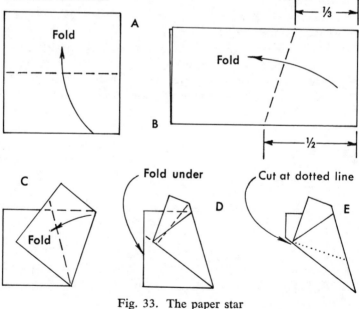

Fig. 33. The paper star

100

THE PAPER STAR

Take a large piece of white newsprint that is perfectly square in size and fold and cut as shown in figure 33. The exact size of the paper should be determined by the size of the audience. The important thing in this paper tear is that it must be a *square* piece of paper and that the fold, as shown in figure 33*b,* is done correctly. Fold the paper at an angle, as shown, with the bottom end of the fold at half the width of the paper and the top edge at one third of the width of the paper. This fold is critical if the star is to have perfect form.

HEAVEN AND HELL

To demonstrate how paper-cutting or tearing can be used as sermon illustrations, I would like to include in this chapter a sermon in paper cutting, entitled, "Heaven and Hell." The text for the sermon is taken from 2 Peter 3:9. This is a marvelous way to show through paper-cutting that the way of redemption is by way of the cross of Christ.

Using the text as the basis for the sermon, at the proper moment, fold and cut the paper to form a cross. The leftover pieces from the cutting out of the cross are used to form the word *hell* and the altar and candles for the cross. Later, the same leftover pieces that were used to form the word *hell* are used to form the word *life.*

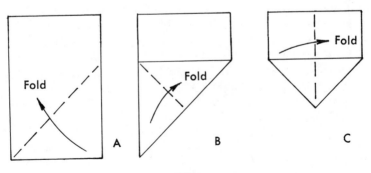

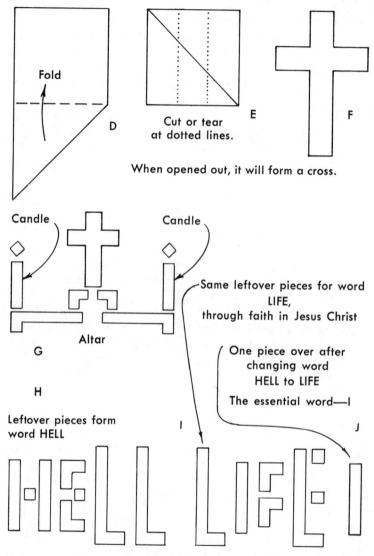

Fold

Cut or tear
at dotted lines.

D

E

F

When opened out, it will form a cross.

Candle

Candle

Same leftover pieces for word
LIFE,
through faith in Jesus Christ

Altar

G

One piece over after
changing word
HELL to LIFE

The essential word—I

H

Leftover pieces form
word HELL

I

J

Fig. 34. The tears for "Heaven and Hell"

When you have done this, the audience will immediately notice that you have one extra piece. You then hold it up and proceed to tell them that the leftover piece stands for the word *I*. Salvation is a personal matter and only, as an individual, can one decide whether or not he or she will accept Christ as Saviour and Lord. This is a very graphic way of demonstrating the plan of salvation by paper-cutting. I'm sure other ideas will come to you with reference to the other paper tears.

SUGGESTIONS FOR USING PAPER TEARS AS SERMONS

To assist you in thinking through how some of the paper tears might be used to illustrate biblical truths, I would like to share with you some texts and suggestions for certain of the paper tears given in this chapter.

The pilot wheel is a wonderful paper tear to illustrate Psalm 32:8. A pilot's wheel is used to steer and guide great ships on their course across the ocean. Jesus Christ is our Pilot. When we come to Him in faith and entrust our lives to His care, we need not fear for He will guide us safely to our destination. The appeal of the sermon should be that each individual should allow Christ to become the Pilot of his life.

The expanding card can be used to illustrate 1 Peter 2:2. Show by the use of the expanding card how, what at first may appear to be impossible is possible, if you know the secret. So it is that through faith in Jesus Christ as Master and Lord, we can grow up to full spiritual maturity. The secret of spiritual maturity is that once we have tasted of the kindness of the Lord we want to commit ourselves completely to Him and His will for our lives.

The paper star is a wonderful effect to preach a sermon on Daniel 12:3. The gist is simply, if we are wise, we will commit our lives completely to Christ. We will allow His will to reign in our lives. When we do, we will be a blessing to others. We will shine like the stars in the firmament, and through the testi-

103

mony of our lives many will be won to our Lord and Saviour Jesus Christ and be saved.

The paper tree can be used to illustrate the story of creation as recorded in the book of Genesis. Or it could be used to relate the story of redemption, the emphasis being placed on how Christ bore our sins "in his body on the tree," as recorded in 1 Peter 2:21-24. Two other interesting texts might be Revelation 22: 1-5 on "the tree of life," and Luke 6:43.

The paper ladder is a beautiful way in which to relate the story of Jacob as recorded in Genesis 28.

I hope that these suggestions will stimulate thought and that you will find paper-tearing or cutting a fascinating way to illustrate biblical truths. As you use this method, you will find that children love the mystery of paper-tearing and cutting.

Part IV

USEFUL PROPS

28

EQUIPMENT YOU CAN MAKE

ONE OF THE DRAWBACKS to acquiring good, basic magic equipment is that it is often very expensive. However, there are certain nice-to-have items that you can make with just a little effort. In this chapter I would like to share with you ideas of how you can make equipment with simple tools and materials.

PRODUCTION TUBE

To make a production tube, all you will need is cardboard, wallpaper, a can of dull black paint, scissors, and a sharp knife. A little creative and artistic ability will also help greatly.

To make the large outer tube, you will need a piece of cardboard large enough to form a tube with a diameter of about 6 inches and about 12 inches high (see fig. 35a). I use the word *about* because the dimensions can be altered to meet your own situation. They should be determined by whether you desire to produce a lot or a little from the tube.

The tube is simply made of the cardboard which is bent to shape and glued at the joint. It is then covered with wallpaper or adhesive paper, preferably the type with a mass of small designs. A border of wallpaper is also put on either end of the tube (see fig. 35a). The inside of the tube is painted a dull black. Two holes approximately 2½ inches in diameter are then cut through the tube, one above the other, as in figure 35a.

A second tube is also required. It is the same height as the

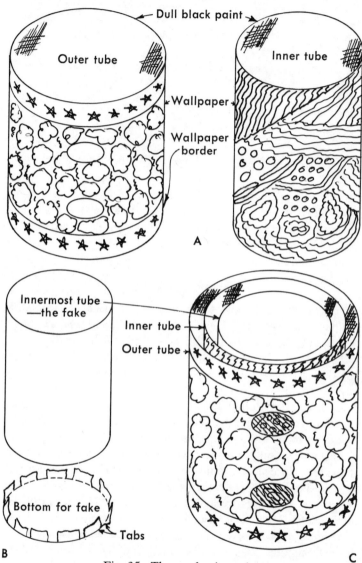

Fig. 35. The production tube

outer tube but should be ½ inch smaller in diameter, so as to fit into the outer tube. There are no holes cut in this tube; it remains solid. It would be best to cover this piece of cardboard with a different design of wallpaper, if possible. The same type paper can be used, but the tubes will look more professional if a different type paper is used to cover the inner tube. That way it will show through the holes in the outer tube. It also is painted a dull black on the inside.

The fake is a third tube made from cardboard. It should be approximately 9 inches high and 5 inches in diameter. It is made to fit into the inner tube. It must also have a bottom. This can be made from a circle of cardboard with tabs cut in it and folded up and glued to the inside of the fake (see fig. 35b). This tube should be painted dull black on both the outside and inside.

To work the effect, the tubes are nested together; the load for the production is in the innermost of the three tubes, inside the fake with the bottom to it (see fig. 35c). First show that the outer tube is empty by taking it off and showing it to the audience. Then replace it over the inner tube. Now remove the inner tube, leaving the fake in the outer tube. Show it to be empty. Replace it in the outer tube and produce the load from the innermost tube, the fake.

See figure 35c, which will explain how the three tubes are nested.

PORTABLE MAGIC TABLE

It is essential that anyone performing magic have some type of portable table to carry with him when he is asked to perform in another church or auditorium. Don't take for granted that they'll have just the type table you need. The chances are they won't. Also it is important to have a table that is uniquely yours and is impressive in appearance. A very nice, collapsible table can be made from an old music stand. Discard the top rod and music holder and use only the lower part of the tripod. Make the top out of ¾-inch plywood 10 inch × 18 inch. Round off

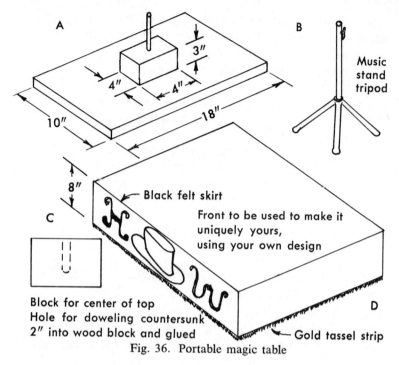

Fig. 36. Portable magic table

Labels within figure:
A

B — Music stand tripod

3″

4″   4″

10″   18″

8″

C — Black felt skirt

Front to be used to make it uniquely yours, using your own design

Block for center of top
Hole for doweling countersunk
2″ into wood block and glued

D — Gold tassel strip

the corners and edges, and, underneath, screw a block of wood 4 inch × 4 inch × 3 inch into the center of plywood top (see fig. 36a).

In this piece of wood, drill a hole to take a piece of doweling 6 inches long, which should be glued into the block of wood (see fig. 36c). Make sure the diameter of the doweling is large enough to fit firmly into the top shaft of the music stand tripod. If it is not, the top will tend to wobble.

Take a piece of black felt material and make a skirt to go around the front and two sides of the tabletop (see fig. 36d). It should be at least eight inches wide. Add a piece of gold tassel to the bottom edge to dress it up. You may also wish to use gold material to dress up the front of the skirt with a top hat, rabbit, initials, or anything that will make it uniquely *yours*. Be sure to glue a piece of felt on the entire top of the table, completely covering it. This will help reduce the noise when effects are being performed.

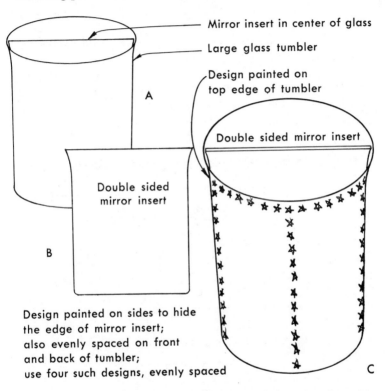

Mirror insert in center of glass

Large glass tumbler

Design painted on top edge of tumbler

A

Double sided mirror insert

Double sided mirror insert

B

Design painted on sides to hide the edge of mirror insert; also evenly spaced on front and back of tumbler; use four such designs, evenly spaced

C

Fig. 37. Production mirror glass

PRODUCTION MIRROR GLASS

There is a very useful tumbler on the market with a metal insert which enables it to look empty from the viewpoint of the audience, while the other side is loaded with whatever you wish to produce.

109

Make a larger version by getting the largest glass you can. Then cut a cardboard form that will fit the center of the glass tightly. Take it down to a mirror shop and have them make you a center for the glass from a scrap piece of double-sided mirror. Glue the double-sided mirror into position, as shown in figure 37a.

Where the edge of the mirror might be visible to the audience, paint a strip design down the sides and in the front and back. Also paint a design around the top of the glass, as in figure 37c.

Once you have this piece of equipment, numerous ideas for its use will come to mind. It is a handy piece of magical equipment to have on hand.

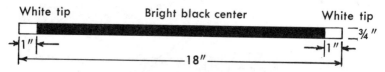

Fig. 38. Magic wand

MAGIC WAND

A nice magic wand can be made from a ¾-inch piece of doweling eighteen inches long. Paint the wand a bright black color. Then, 1 inch on either end, paint a tip bright white. This is a piece of equipment you will use all the time. So take the necessary time to do a good job in painting it. In order to get the tips painted on correctly use masking tape to get a good, neat border.

When performing, always have a magic wand handy. It is one of the major tools of a professional magician. The audience expects to see it!

VANISHING BOX

A vanishing box is a very important piece of magic equipment, because there are many times that some item in an effect must be made to disappear. This box is a wonderful piece of apparatus to bring about this effect in a professional manner.

110

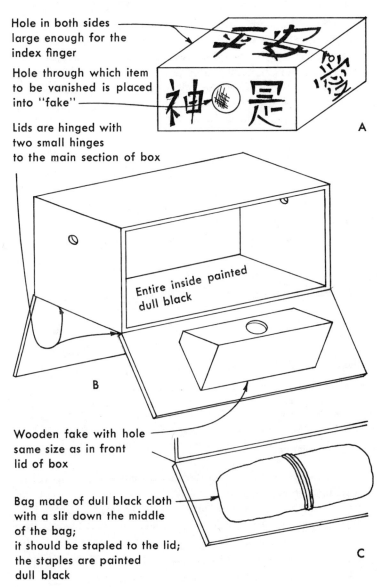

Hole in both sides large enough for the index finger

Hole through which item to be vanished is placed into "fake"

Lids are hinged with two small hinges to the main section of box

A

Entire inside painted dull black

B

Wooden fake with hole same size as in front lid of box

Bag made of dull black cloth with a slit down the middle of the bag; it should be stapled to the lid; the staples are painted dull black

C

It should be made from either ¼ inch or ⅜ inch plywood. The dimensions of the box will vary and should be determined by its use. If it is to be used simply to vanish silks, then it should be small in size. If, on the other hand, it is to be used to vanish larger items, then it should be built with dimensions necessary to accomplish the mission you have in mind. It can be built either with a wooden fake, as in figure 39*b* or with a larger cloth fake, as in figure 39*c*.

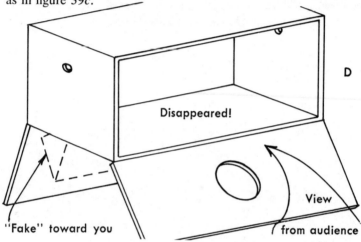

Fig. 39. Vanishing box

The box, when completed, should be painted on the outside with a bright color, preferably red or yellow, with some type of Oriental design, in contrasting color, as in figure 39*a*. The inside of the box is painted a dull black.

To use the box, simply put the silk or item you wish to vanish through the hole in the front lid of the box. Be sure it is completely inside the wooden or cloth fake on the back lid of the box. Then simply flip the box over and allow the two lids to drop down, as in figure 39*d*. The lid with the fake should be toward you and away from the audience. It is a perfect effect for a complete vanish of any item.

PRODUCTION BOX

This is a clever production box for making things magically appear before the people's eyes. By simply pulling on the cords, a dove, silks, and so on, appear in the opening at the front of the box. It would be well worth the effort and time to build this production box for use in certain of your sermons in magic.

It should be made from either ¼ inch or ⅜ inch plywood. Paint it on the outside either a bright red, green, or yellow. The Oriental design at the top of the front panel (see fig. 40a) should

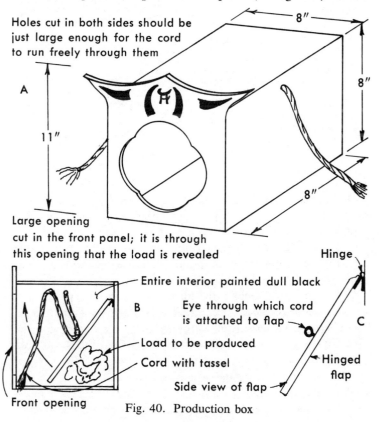

Holes cut in both sides should be just large enough for the cord to run freely through them

A

11″

8″

8″

8″

Large opening cut in the front panel; it is through this opening that the load is revealed

Entire interior painted dull black

B

Eye through which cord is attached to flap

Load to be produced

Cord with tassel

Side view of flap

Front opening

Hinge

C

Hinged flap

Fig. 40. Production box

113

be painted a contrasting color, such as red-colored box with yellow design. The interior of the box should be a dull black. The cord should be at least ¼ inch in diameter, preferably gold in color with tassels on both ends.

The diagrams in figure 40 should be sufficient to assist you in building the production box. The dimensions are only recommended size. They can be varied to meet your specific needs.

Piece of cardboard
fitting tightly
in top of hat

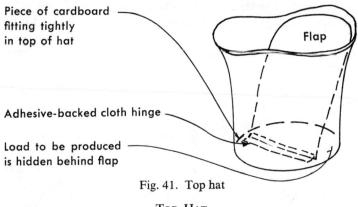

Flap

Adhesive-backed cloth hinge

Load to be produced
is hidden behind flap

Fig. 41. Top hat

TOP HAT

A black top hat has long been one of the symbols of a professional magician. So if you would like to take on more of a professional look, purchase a cheap top hat and make it into a production item. It can be done easily with the use of a couple pieces of cardboard, a small piece of adhesive-backed cloth, and some dull black paint.

Cut a piece of cardboard to fit tightly in the top of the hat. Then cut another piece of cardboard to make the flap (see fig. 41). Attach the flap to the other piece of cardboard with the adhesive-backed cloth. Paint the cardboard dull black on both sides. Then fit it into the hat.

By simply holding the flap against the side of the brim with the right hand, quickly show the inside of the hat as you exchange it from the right to the left hand. The load to be produced from the hat is hidden behind the flap. As the left hand receives the hat, the flap will have been released by the right hand. Merely grab the flap with the left hand and pull it to the other side of the hat. The items to be produced will now be revealed.

UTILITY STAND

As you progress in your knowledge of magic, you will find that a nice utility stand will come in handy. Among the numerous uses for such a stand would be: (1) to hold a crossbar, on which to hang production items so that your audience can see the quantity of items produced from a small production box; (2) to hold a large piece of cardboard, especially for sermons in chemical magic; (3) to hold a framed picture; (4) to hold a cardboard sign with your name on it, or a passage of Scripture which is the theme of your sermon in magic; or (5) to hold a

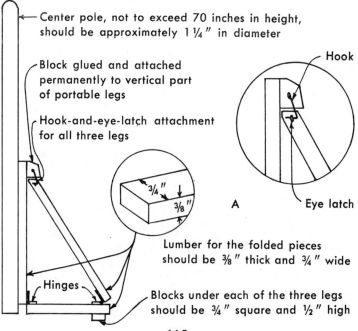

← Center pole, not to exceed 70 inches in height, should be approximately 1 ¼ ″ in diameter

Block glued and attached permanently to vertical part of portable legs

Hook-and-eye-latch attachment for all three legs

Hook

¾ ″
⅜ ″

A

Eye latch

Lumber for the folded pieces should be ⅜ ″ thick and ¾ ″ wide

Hinges

Blocks under each of the three legs should be ¾ ″ square and ½ ″ high

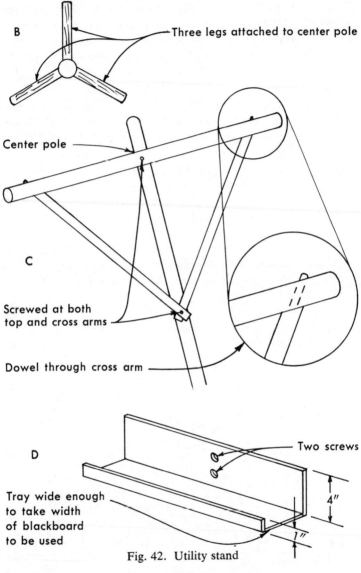

B — Three legs attached to center pole

Center pole

C

Screwed at both top and cross arms

Dowel through cross arm

D

Two screws

Tray wide enough to take width of blackboard to be used

4"

1"

Fig. 42. Utility stand

116

blackboard to write the important points in your sermon that you wish to drive home.

The important thing in making such a large utility item is that it must be portable. Everything you use in sermons in magic should be able to fit in the family car or station wagon. That's why I believe you'll find these plans to be such that you'll want to make and use this type utility stand.

Three legs to the stand should be identical, as explained in figure 42a. When assembling for performance, they should be screwed to the center pole with two screws each. They should be evenly spaced around the center pole, as in figure 42b.

Accessories for the utility stand should include a crossbar made of ¾ inch dowel with two crossarms. When used, it should be screwed to the center pole by two screws in order to make it secure. The crossbar is illustrated in figure 42c.

In order to hold a blackboard or piece of cardboard, a shelf must be made. It should be made from ⅜ inch lumber, and two screws must be used to secure it to the center pole.

29

SERVANTE AND BLACK ART WELL

BOTH THE ABILITY to make an object vanish and appear magically are essential to the good performance of magic. So I would
like to share with you in this chapter some basic professional
methods for doing both.

Two very basic conjurer's props for vanishing an item are
the servante and the black art well. The servante is nothing more
than a small shelf attached to the back of the magic table being
used. It can vary in size and shape. Two basic types of servantes
are shown in figure 43.

As you can see, if there is a nice cloth fringe around the front

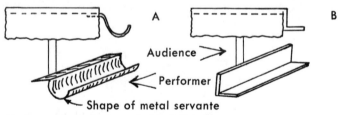

This type of servante is made
from a small piece of metal
bent to shape and covered with
a piece of black felt or velvet.
It is attached with screws to the
back underside of the tabletop

This type of servante is made
from a small piece of lumber
and two simple stantions,
which attach it to the back of
the tabletop. The shelf should
be covered with black felt or
velvet

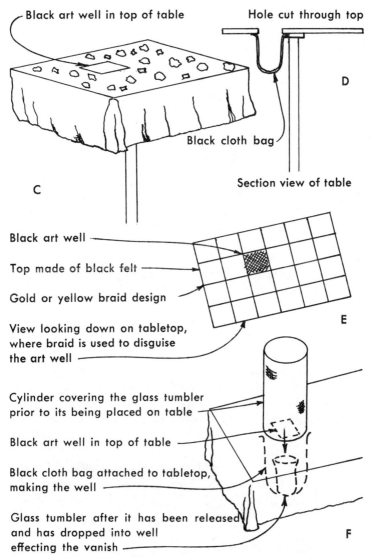

Black art well in top of table

Hole cut through top

Black cloth bag

D

Section view of table

C

Black art well

Top made of black felt

Gold or yellow braid design

View looking down on tabletop,
where braid is used to disguise
the art well

E

Cylinder covering the glass tumbler
prior to its being placed on table

Black art well in top of table

Black cloth bag attached to tabletop,
making the well

Glass tumbler after it has been released
and has dropped into well
effecting the vanish

F

Fig. 43. The servante and black art well

119

and sides of the tabletop, the servante cannot be seen from the audience. It is very important that the servante is not as low hanging as the bottom edge of the cloth fringe around the tabletop. Also, when using a servante, be sure to check the audience angle with reference to the placing of the table, as explained in chapter 2, "Arranging a Room or Auditorium."

To illustrate how a servante can be utilized, let's suppose that you had an object which you wanted to disappear from your closed right hand. All you would need to do is, as you reach to pick up your magic wand to assist you in making the object disappear, under the action of picking up the magic wand, you simply lower your right hand momentarily behind the table and release the object and let it drop on the servante. This is why it is so essential to have the servante well padded with felt or velvet, so as not to let the dropped object "talk," that is, make any audible sound when dropped to the servante.

The black art well is simply a hole cut through the top of the table with a black cloth bag hanging from it. When using a well, be sure the top of the table is covered with black felt. This way the opening is not seen except for those who might examine the top close up.

To further conceal the black art well from the audience, a design made of gold or yellow braid does a fine job. Be sure that the black cloth bag does not hang below the lower edge of the cloth fringe around the front and sides of the tabletop. The size of the well opening and bag would depend on what objects you were planning to vanish. Figure 43 illustrates some black art wells.

A black art well can be used to cause glass tumblers, silks, and even rather bulky articles to disappear by simply covering them with a cylinder or other object. Then, while holding the object through the top of the cylinder, place it momentarily on the table over the well. Release the object, and it will silently disappear into the well. Then just pick up the cylinder and show that it is empty. See the illustration in figure 43e.

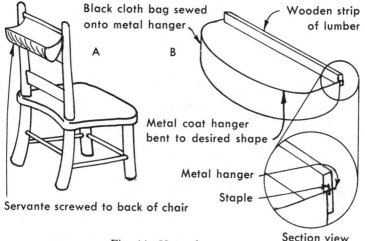

Black cloth bag sewed onto metal hanger

A

B

Wooden strip of lumber

Metal coat hanger bent to desired shape

Metal hanger

Staple

Servante screwed to back of chair

Section view

Fig. 44. Uses of a servante

A servante can also be very useful in producing an object. It can be attached not only to the back of a table for this use, but a very handy one can be attached to back of chair which is used merely as a prop. The chair, if one is to be used for this purpose, should be wooden, with a thick top rail across the back, as illustrated in figure 44*a*.

The servante can also be made simply from a strip of lumber, a coat hanger, and some black cloth. This type of servante is easy to make and can be used either for vanishing or producing an object. It can be used on the back of a chair, a table, or even a wooden tray.

A servante attached to the back of a chair can be easily used unnoticed by the audience. In the process of leaning a hand on the back of the chair, an object placed in the servante can be taken up without drawing attention to it in any way.

Another method of using a chair for picking up a large, bulky load for a production is by simply using the same chair as illustrated in figure 44. However, instead of a servante, use only a large eye hook screwed to the back of the top wooden panel on

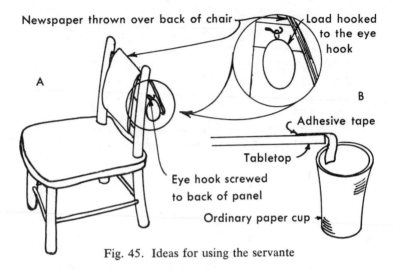

Newspaper thrown over back of chair

Load hooked to the eye hook

A

B

Adhesive tape

Tabletop

Eye hook screwed to back of panel

Ordinary paper cup

Fig. 45. Ideas for using the servante

the back of the chair. A wonderful way to assist in the production can be the use of a newspaper. Show the paper on both sides, then momentarily place it over the back of the chair. At the proper moment, scoop up the object, which is already wrapped in newspaper, tied with a string and hooked on the eye hook, as the paper is crumbled together. Tear open the newspaper and from the center of it produce the object. This is really a clean and effective method of producing an object.

Another great idea for a servante for small objects that can be done on the spur of the moment is to simply use a large paper cup taped to the back of a chair or table.

Another clever way to produce an item is by use of a top hat. Simply attach a small hook to the brim of the hat. The object to be produced has a piece of black cotton string attached to it. It is placed in the servante on the back of your magic table with the loop in the string sticking upward. The hat with the hook toward the servante is placed on the table brim down (see fig. 46a). When it is picked up from the table, simply slide it back so that the hook can engage the loop attached to the load. The hat is then turned over on its top, and the load produced. The hat should be turned over as illustrated in figure 46b.

These are just a few good, professional ideas that I feel you will find most useful as you branch out in the area of sermons in magic. You will find many uses for a servante and black art well; so do give a lot of thought to their use.

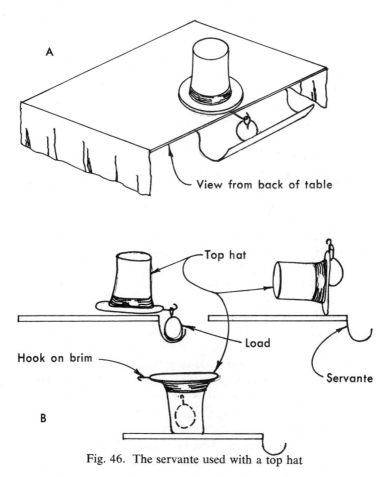

Fig. 46. The servante used with a top hat

CONCLUSION

A LAST WORD, PLEASE

YOU NOW HAVE in your possession the secrets to a number of professional magic effects. Let me urge you to practice them faithfully before you attempt to use them. Be sure to follow the instructions carefully both in the construction of each effect and its use. Please do not rush into doing any of these effects. They may at first glance appear to be simple, but I can assure you that if you have not practiced to the extent that all of your moves are natural, you will foul up and give the secret of the effect away. Once this has happened, you can be sure the effectiveness of your message will be lost. This is important! For after all, the purpose of sermons in magic is to present the Good News. Therefore, let me stress this point: PRACTICE, PRACTICE, PRACTICE, until every move becomes a part of you. Everything that we do in the presentation of the glorious truths of the Word of God is worth our very best.

I am sure that, as you have read this book, you have been motivated to want to go on and develop magical sermons of your own. Let me encourage you to do this. You will find it to be both challenging and gratifying. You may wish to look into purchasing other pieces of professional magic equipment. If so, look in your telephone directory; you might be surprised to find that there is a magic dealer right in your own town. If so, go by and visit with him. You will find him to be friendly and helpful. Have him demonstrate for you some of the magic effects you feel you might be interested in. This way you will be sure of what you are buying and what will be useful in your work.

I might also suggest that if there is not a magic dealer close to where you live, you might secure two or three magic catalogs from magic houses to browse through for ideas. However, let me urge you not to rush into buying too much expensive equipment. When you find an effect that you feel might be adaptable to a biblical message, first talk with someone who has been doing this type of work before you purchase it. Don't hesitate to ask advice! You will find that most magicians are happy to be of help to someone just starting out.

Another area where you can find help is your local library. Check out some books on magic. In these books you will find many magical effects which you can build with just a little effort and expense. An excellent library of books on magic is *The Tarbell Course in Magic* by Harlan Tarbell. There are seven volumes in the set, and it is a library on professional magic that everyone who is serious in his quest for knowledge about magic should own. It can be purchased from Louis Tannen, 120 West 42nd Street, New York, N. Y. 10036.

If you look around, you will be amazed at the tremendous wealth of material on magic that is available. However, be on guard against the magic bug biting you to the extent that you begin to waste money on flashy, expensive and often useless equipment. It is *not* necessary to have a lot of flashy and expensive equipment in order to do effective sermons in magic. Always keep foremost in your mind that it is the *message* that is important. The *only* purpose for the magic effect is to illustrate your message.

If there is not a magic dealer close to where you reside, you may wish to secure a catalog either from Louis Tannen, whose address is mentioned above, or from the Top Hat Magic Company, 1007 Davis Street, Evanston, Illinois 60201. I have found both of these magic dealers to be reputable.

I pray that you will find doing these sermons in magic both enjoyable and spiritually rewarding. If you have been blessed through your ministry in magic, do share your experiences with me. I would be most happy to hear from you.

In closing, let me urge you to present your magic in a worshipful manner. May your one desire in using the magic presented in this book be that of winning some lost person to our Lord and Saviour Jesus Christ, who is the way, the truth, and the life. May God richly bless your ministry.